MORE THAN A HASHTAG

MORE THAN A HASHTAG

Facing the Reality That Our Lives Matter

MICHAEL AGER

RICH HABITS PUBLISHING
Richmond, Virginia

ISBN (Paperback): 9781540388407

Contents

Introduction

Imagine having dinner with your family. Imagine someone force-fully kicking down your door with weapons brandished, speaking a foreign language, dressed in clothes you have never seen, faces and complexions you have never seen, looking at you with hate and disgust in their eyes and proceeding to throw a net over you and continuously beat you. Imagine seeing your wife and children beat on and dragged in separate directions, while you are taken in another direction with no way to stop it. Imagine being shackled in the bottom of a large ship and carried with 250 to 600 others in a space that you can barely turn in, not being fed, and beaten for six to thirteen weeks not knowing where you were going. Imagine lying on a wet floor in unbearable heat in a space about five feet three inches high and four feet four inches wide. Finally, as your trip ends and you have some hope that you may live and see your family again, you are taken off the ship by strangers, washed, shaved, and rubbed with palm oil to disguise the bruises, sores, and cuts caused by the ship's conditions. The land looks strange, the people look strange, and the fear of not knowing what lies ahead consumes you. As the neck and feet shackles dig into your skin, leaving marks that will never go away, you are placed on an auction block, where you are inspected head to toe like cattle, or dogs at a pound waiting to be adopted. Any bond you may have made with other people who were captured when you were is now broken as you are thrown into the back of a wagon by your new owner. In this free world, where we were put here as humans to serve one master—above—you will now serve a new master, a human master, who will obliterate the identities of his newly acquired slaves. He will break your will and sever any bonds with the past, issue you a new name, teach you a new language, a new religion, force you to work all day for free, and punish you whenever he feels the need. There are daily reminders to keep you in fear and to remain in bondage, such as a burnt body hanging from a noose strung up in a tree, or the permanent scars on someone's back from being whipped to a bloody pulp for making eye contact. You are denied a bath for weeks and forced to eat slop with your bare hands, bloody and dirty from working the fields all day.

1

'Bout That Life

Slave life varied greatly depending on many factors. Life in the fields meant working sunup to sundown six days a week and having food sometimes not suitable for an animal to eat. Plantation slaves lived in small shacks with a dirt floor and little or no furniture. Life on large plantations with a cruel overseer was oftentimes the worst. However, work for a small farm owner who was not doing well could mean not being fed. The stories about cruel overseers were certainly true in some cases. The overseer was paid to get the most work out of the slaves; therefore, overseers often resorted to whatever means was necessary. Sometimes the slaves would drive the overseer off the plantation in desperation. When slaves complained that they were being unfairly treated, slaveholders would most often be very protective of their "property" and would release the overseer. In some cases, a driver was used rather than an overseer. The difference between the overseer and the driver was simple: drivers were slaves themselves. A driver

---

might be convinced by a master to manage the slaves for better privileges. The rest of the slaves usually hated drivers. These feelings often led to violence.

Large plantations often required some slaves to work in the plantation home. These slaves enjoyed far better circumstances. Domestic slaves lived in better quarters and received better food. They sometimes were able to travel with the owner's family. In many cases, a class system developed within the slave community. Domestic slaves did not often associate themselves with plantation slaves. They often aspired to arrange courtships for their children with other domestic slaves. As the "peculiar institution" spread across the South, many states passed "slave codes," which outlined the rights of slaves and the acceptable treatment and rules regarding slaves. Slave codes varied from state to state, but there were many common threads. One could not do business with a slave without the prior consent of the owner. Slaves could be awarded as prizes in raffles, wagered in gambling, offered as security for loans, and transferred as gifts from one person to another. A slave was not permitted to keep a gun. If caught carrying a gun, the slave received 39 lashes and forfeited the gun. Blacks were held incompetent as witnesses in legal cases involving whites. The education of slaves was prohibited. Anyone operating a school or teaching reading and writing to any African American in Missouri could be punished by a fine of not less than $500 and up to six months in jail. Slaves could not assemble without a white person present. Marriages between slaves were not considered legally binding. Therefore, owners were free to split up families through sale.

Any slave found guilty of arson, rape of a white woman, or conspiracy to rebel was put to death. However, since the slave woman was chattel, a white man who raped her was guilty only of a trespass on the master's property. Rape was common on the plantation, and very few cases were ever reported.

Some masters made slaves fight to the death, for entertainment. This process was called "seasoning," and it went on for two to three years. If you were lucky enough to take the trip with your family, you would watch as this new master raped your wife and beat or killed your children if he felt they were useless. Most slaves lived on large farms or small plantations; many masters owned less than 50 slaves. Slave owners sought to make their slaves completely dependent on them, and a system of restrictive codes governed life among slaves. They were prohibited from learning to read and write, and their behavior and movement was restricted. Many masters took sexual liberties with slave women and rewarded obedient slave behavior with favors, while rebellious slaves were brutally punished. A strict hierarchy among slaves (from privileged house slaves and skilled artisans down to lowly field hands) helped keep them divided and less likely to organize against their masters. Slave marriages had no legal basis, but slaves did marry and raise large families; most slave owners encouraged this practice but nonetheless did not hesitate to divide slave families by sale or removal. Enslaved people were valued at every stage of their lives, from before birth until after death. Slaveholders examined women for their fertility and projected the value of their "future increase." As they grew up, enslavers assessed their value through a rating system that quantified their work. An "A1 Prime Hand" was a term used for a "first rate" slave who could do the most work in a given day. Their values decreased on a quarter scale from three-fourths hands to one-fourth hands, to a rate of zero, which was typically reserved for elderly or differently abled bond people (another term for slaves.) For Africans weakened by the trauma of the voyage, the brutality of this process was overwhelming. Many died or committed suicide. Others resisted and were punished. The rest found ways of appearing to conform that still preserved their dignity. If you are thinking to yourself, where could this happen? How can people be so cruel and inhumane, totally disregarding the humans rights of others for capital gain?

2

Welcome to AMERICA

In the early 17th century, European settlers in North America
turned to African slaves as a cheaper, more plentiful labor source
than indentured servants (who were mostly poorer Europeans).
After 1619, when a Dutch ship brought 20 Africans ashore at the
British colony of Jamestown, Virginia, slavery spread throughout
the American colonies. Though it is impossible to give accurate
figures, some historians have estimated that six to seven million
slaves were imported to the New World during the 18th century
alone, depriving the African continent of some of its healthiest
and ablest men and women. In the pre-Civil War United States, a
stronger case can be made that slavery played a critical role in economic development. One crop, slave-grown cotton, provided over
half of all US export earnings. By 1840, the South was growing
60% of the world's cotton and provided some 70% of the cotton
consumed by the British textile industry. Thus slavery paid for
a substantial share of the capital, iron, and manufactured goods

that laid the basis for American economic growth. In addition, precisely because the South specialized in cotton production, the North developed a variety of businesses that provided services for the slave South, including textile factories, a meat processing industry, insurance companies, shippers, and cotton brokers.

3

Labor Pangs

———————

In America, some argue that the slave trade lasted anywhere from 265 to 400 years, depending on the definition, but none argue the fact that the profit made off of free black labor was bigger than wall street itself. It is no secret that slavery rests at the foundation of American capitalism and is often synonymous with the sugar, tobacco, and/or cotton plantations that fueled the southern economy. What many may not know is that slavery also rests at the foundation of many notable corporations. From New York Life to Bank of America, several companies have benefitted from slavery. Many of the companies even acknowledged their involvement in slavery and offered apologies in an attempt to reconcile their tainted history; but, is an apology enough? History has consistently shown that slavery has diminished the quality of life for African Americans and simultaneously enhanced the quality of life for white Americans. From institutionalized racism to blocked social and economic opportunities, African Americans are often excluded of African Americans. Apologies cannot compensate an entire race of people for all of the social and economic ills they face as a result of their enslavement. They cannot address the residual effects of slavery. They cannot provide job opportunities to a race of people who are experiencing high unemployment rates—that is, apologies without action from the very systems slave labor helped to create. Had it not been for slave labor, many corporations would not be where they are today, and for these companies to acknowledge their involvement in slavery and then simply say, *Oh, we're sorry* is to downplay their role in perpetuating the degradation and nothing more than a futile attempt to correct a wrong by pacifying the wronged. Instead of apologies, these companies could give back to the African American community by donating to historically black colleges and universities (HBCUs), investing in minority businesses, offering more minority scholarships, or launching initiatives to increase their number of minority employees. Corporations who profited from slavery still exist, Tiffany & Co. was originally financed with profits from a Connecticut cotton mill worked by slaves, Aetna and AIG insured the lives of slaves and reimbursed slave owners when they died, and Bank of America and Wachovia accepted slaves as collateral on loans—just to name a few. Economists and historians have examined detailed aspects of the enslaved experience for as long as slavery existed. Recent publications related to slavery and capitalism explore economic aspects of cotton production and offer commentary on the amount of wealth generated from enslaved labor. My own work enters this conversation by looking at the value of individual slaves and the ways enslaved people responded to being treated as a commodity. They were bought and sold just like we sell cars and cattle today. They were gifted, deeded, and mortgaged the same way we sell houses today. They were itemized and insured the same way we manage our assets and protect our valuables. Slavery was an extremely diverse economic institution, one that extrapolated unpaid labor out of people in a variety of settings from small single crop farms and plantations to urban universities. This diversity is also reflected in their prices. Enslaved people understood they were treated as commodities. Furthermore, slaves could not be granted patents for any inventions that they created until after the Civil War. As a result, the efforts of slaves were ignored or, if accepted, credited to their masters.

After years of tolerance by blacks, some whites began to grow a conscience, or began to think of bigger ways to profit from these hard working people. Revolts began to grow in the mid-1800s, and slaves began to fight back via leaders in the North, such as Frederick Douglass, and organized revolts led by Nat Turner. Some managed to escape by any means necessary, especially through Harriett Tubman and the Underground Railroad. In the mid-19th century, while the United States was experiencing an era of tremendous growth, a fundamental economic difference existed between the country's northern and southern regions. While in the North, manufacturing and industry was well established, and agriculture was mostly limited to small-scale farms, the South's economy was based on a system of large-scale farming that depended on the labor of black slaves to grow certain crops, especially cotton and tobacco. The growing abolitionist sentiment in the North after the 1830s and northern opposition to slavery's extension into the new western territories led many southerners to fear that the existence of slavery in America—and thus the backbone of their economy—was in danger.

4

Free at Last?

Enter president Abraham Lincoln, who became president in March of 1861 and drafted the Emancipation Proclamation on January 1, 1863, which freed the slaves of the Confederate states after pressure from white non-slave owners who could not get work due to the competition from free labor by slaves. Lincoln had used the occasion of the Union victory at Antietam to issue a preliminary Emancipation Proclamation, which freed all slaves in the rebellious states after January 1, 1863. He justified his decision as a wartime measure and did not go so far as to free the slaves in the border states loyal to the Union. Still, the Emancipation Proclamation deprived the Confederacy of the bulk of its labor forces and put international public opinion strongly on the Union side. Some 186,000 black soldiers would join the Union Army by the time the Civil War ended in 1865, and 38,000 lost their lives. The 13th Amendment, adopted late in 1865, officially abolished slavery, but freed blacks' status in the post-war South remained precarious, and significant challenges awaited during the Reconstruction period (1865–77). Former slaves received the rights of citizenship and the "equal protection" of the Constitution in the 14th Amendment (1868) and the right to vote in the 15th (1870), but the provisions of the Constitution were often ignored or violated, and it was difficult for former slaves to gain a foothold in the postwar economy thanks to restrictive black codes and regressive contractual arrangements such as sharecropping. Once slaves were so-called "free"—after hundreds of years of being taught to envy each other, hate each other, be inferior to whites, speak and act and think white, pray white, learn white language, and all without any compensation—what was to be done? If you put three million people in jail, have them raised there, die there, raise families there, for four generations, and all of a sudden one day you open the gates and say you guys are free...what do you think will happen? They will live the only way they know how, and that is survival mode. This is exactly what happened. The American Government also knew this would happen; they wanted it to happen. They basically replaced the name slave with the word prisoner. Once you look deep into the 13th Amendment, it is easy to see. The 13th Amendment to the U.S. Constitution officially abolished slavery in America, and was ratified on December 6, 1865, after the conclusion of the American Civil War. The amendment states: "Neither slavery nor involuntary servitude, except as a punishment for crime whereof the party shall have been duly convicted, shall exist within the United States, or any place subject to their jurisdiction." The government knew the freed slaves would have to either choose to stay with their masters or be free and commit crimes to eat and survive. You would think that a government who released slaves into freedom would have done so because they realized it was wrong to enslave humans for profit, for we were all born with inalienable rights by God. Unfortunately, this wasn't the case. *How can we make this operation even bigger?* they said. *Hmmm; we have to make sure this doesn't come back to hit us in the pockets. Now that the slaves are freed with no compensation for hundreds of years of work, how can we legally make this okay?*

5

Amendments

———————

Following its ratification by the necessary three-quarters of U.S. states, the 14th Amendment, guaranteeing to African Americans citizenship and all its privileges, was officially adopted into the U.S. Constitution. Why is this important? *Let's make all of the freed slaves citizens, so we will never have to pay any reparations.* The simple definition of reparations is the making of amends for a wrong one has done, by paying money to or otherwise helping those who have been wronged. You cannot receive reparations if you are a citizen; it is the same as if you work for a company: you cannot sue that company while you are employed there. Unlike the Jews, who received reparations for the Holocaust, and the Native Americans, who do not have to pay taxes, African Americans didn't receive one penny for hundreds of years of work, where America profited off of free labor. After the Civil War, the 13th, 14th, and 15th Constitutional amendments were passed, which aided newly freed slaves in being treated equally under the law, or so the story goes. The fact of the matter is that slavery was—and still is—completely legal in the United States, and, not only that, but it took on a much different form. The institution of slavery changed in that instead of having the direct enslavement of blacks with an entire apparatus that had to be created to keep slaves in their condition, elements of the state apparatus were used to enslave blacks—namely the legal and prison systems. Yet, the enslavement itself was changed, as black convicts were no longer slaves to individual masters but rather they were enslaved to the companies that they were leased out to. To create this system, there not only had to be the involvement of the southern judicial system and individual northern and southern elites but also the involvement of the corporations and the reinstitution of slavery within a corporate context.

To attain a full understanding of the convict lease system, there must first be a reexamination of the 13th Amendment. It has been stated in history books and in classrooms across America that this amendment ended slavery, yet this is quite false. The 13th Amendment states, "neither slavery nor involuntary servitude, **except as a punishment for crime whereof the party shall have been duly convicted**, shall exist within the United States, or any place subject to their jurisdiction." Thus, slavery is completely and totally legal if it is part (or the whole) of a punishment for someone who was convicted of a crime.

When debating the 13th Amendment, many in Congress were not thinking of slaves but rather white labor, with Senator Henry Wilson saying, "The same influences that go to keep down and crush down the rights of the poor black man bear down and oppress the poor white laboring man." Senator Richard Yates of Illinois was much blunter, stating that he had "never had the negro on the brain" when discussing the amendment. Such notions are absurd! Wilson is correct to an extent when he argues that both slave and white labor are oppressed by the same system; both are oppressed in that they are being manipulated and played off one another by the elite of both the North and South. Still, Wilson ignores the fact that white labor was *very* much less oppressed than black slave labor, as white laborers were seen as human beings, deserving of dignity and respect, rather than treated worse than animals. White laborers were free to do as they pleased, not having to worry about ensuring that they consistently had papers on their person so as to prove their freedom.

The passing of the 13th Amendment should be examined within the context of an economic competition between black slave labor and free white labor. The South's economy was built around slave labor and the ability to have the slaves produce more than they were "worth," seeing as how slaves were viewed as not just general property but a long-term economic investment that helped the southern plantation elite. Yet, due to the existence of slavery, white labor suffered, as not only did they lose out on the income they were making when slavery was first introduced as well as potential future income, but also white labor was unable to make advances within the South, since slaves provided a source of labor that was less expensive in the long-term.

Senator Henry Williams illustrates these points and other problems that white labor had with slavery. He stated that:

Slavery was evil because it destroyed much of the richest land in the South; it degraded labor and the meaning of labor for poor white working men in the South; it robbed the South of culture by degrading the efforts of laborers; and it allowed southern aristocrats to further insult northern white workers by demeaning their laboring efforts as crabbed and mean. It was the association between labor and slavery in the minds of southern aristocrats that demeaned the efforts of industrious northern laborers. Thus, slavery pulled white workers down in two ways: one, by direct competition with slave labor in the South, and two, by associating all the industrious efforts of workers with those of the degraded slaves.

Thus, the only way for white labor to triumph in their struggle for rights such as a fair wage and regular working hours was through the abolition of slavery. White labor had a direct interest in the nullification of slavery.

Yet, there was a difference of opinion in the minds of southern elites who wanted to continue slavery, but on different terms.

6

Southern Elites

Before discussing the southern elites, one must first examine this within the context of the southern economy after the Civil War. It was utterly in shambles. One could make a solid argument that it had been decimated and demolished in virtually every conceivable way. The entire economy of the South was built upon the institution of slavery and agriculture. With the end of the Civil War, not only was the southern economy damaged by the freeing of black slaves, but also the land was deeply scarred and hurt, thus creating an immediate economic problem. However, among all of this there was an opportunity reorient and reconstruct the economy around a new labor source, as cheap labor would be needed to rebuild the region.

The social order must be examined as well. While the slaves were now free and able to do as they pleased, there was still a deeply embedded racism within the minds of southern whites. Just because blacks had fought in the Civil War did not suddenly mean that the perception of blacks had changed; rather, to the southern elites, they still viewed blacks as inferior and only good for labor, longing to perpetuate the slave system but within a new industrial framework, seeing as how the agricultural framework had been destroyed. This new system was to be found in convict leasing.

The leasing out of state convicts to private hands has its basis in the minds of people such as John T. Milner of Alabama. Milner was no ordinary man; rather, he was a southern elite who "was in the vanguard of that new theory of industrial forced labor," writing in 1859 that "black labor marshaled into the regimented productivity of factory settings would be the key to the economic development of Alabama and the South." Milner's idea of using regimented black labor can be seen in his involvement in a project for the Blue River, a railroad company, in Alabama. In 1859 he issued a plan for the laying of rail in Montgomery, "presenting statistical evidence to demonstrate the potential economic benefit to Montgomery of securing connections with Decatur," a city north of Montgomery. He argued that the Blue River could build its own track in nearby Jones Valley with the use of slave labor. Yet, in Milner's mind, this slave labor had to be managed by whites. He stated, "**A negro who can set a saw, or run a grist mill, or work in a blacksmith shop, can do work as cheaply in a rolling mill,** even now, as white men do at the North, **provided he has an overseer, a southern man, who knows how to manage negroes.**" After the end of the Civil War, Milner's plan changed, but he was convinced that "the future of blacks in America rested on how whites *chose* to manage them." To this end, in the 1870s, he moved with the purpose to acquire the black convict labor that Alabama's prisons were offering up. He took these convicts and put them to work in coalmines, treating them barbarically.

Records of Milner's various mines and slave farms in southern Alabama owned by one of his business partners—a cousin to an investor in the Bibb Steam Mill- tell the stories of black women stripped naked and whipped, of hundreds of men starved, changed, and beaten, of workers perpetually lice-ridden and barely clothed.

Black Americans, many of them former slaves, were essentially re-enslaved but within the context of a corporate structure with an alliance between the state and the corporation. Yet, the judicial system was greatly involved in allowing this to occur, from the laws passed to sheriffs selling of convicts to companies.

7

Justice or "Just Us"?

To allow for the convict lease system to exist and for blacks to be reduced to their former state as a labor source required that the law limit the rights of blacks and criminalize black life to the point that blacks could be imprisoned on the most frivolous of offenses. Such laws took the form of Black Codes.

To understand the creation of Black Codes, it is necessary to understand the social order that motivated elites to push for such legislation. North Carolina is a prime example. After the war, the elite would have preferred the system to revert back to the status quo that existed under the slave system, yet this was not possible due to the liberation of blacks and free whites caused by the destruction of the slave system. This problem was greatly exacerbated by the fact that "in suppressing the war to dissolve the Union the whites were deprived of arms while many Negroes had easily obtained them," thus "A general feeling of insecurity on the part of the whites" resulted. Armed blacks were a threat to elite interests, as, by being able to defend and protect themselves, blacks would be able to ensure that they would not be re-enslaved. Furthermore, it presented a problem to the overall white power structure, as having weapons would empower blacks to stand up for themselves and assert their rights not only as Americans but also as human beings, and such a situation bought the memories and worries of a slave revolt back to the forefront of the minds of elites.

To put blacks back "in their place," the elite pushed several laws that were passed in the state legislature, such as defining "a Negro as any person of African descent, although one ancestor to the fourth generation might be white." The fact that racial identity was dependent on the mother rather than the father made the situation all the worse, as blacks who had white fathers, whether by marriage or by rape, were now considered to be black and thus would be subject to the worst aspects of living within a white supremacist society.

Another example of the law being used to punish blacks were those laws concerning vagrancy. In North Carolina, there was a problem concerning labor as after the Civil War, blacks and whites were working on their own fields, yet many others less energetic, white and black, were flooding the towns and refusing work of any sort, for in the days of bondage, master and slave had been taught that to labor with the hands was undignified: consequently, freedom to many Negroes meant a deliverance from hard labor.

These workers proved a problem to North Carolinian industrialists and agriculturalists, as few could afford to pay workers a wage until the crop had been grown, not to mention that neither employee nor employer were familiar with a wage system. A solution was found in creating vagrancy laws. Of the workers who refused to do any labor, vagrancy laws were passed that stated that a person who had no means of survival or refused to work would be regarded a vagrant and sent to court; however, a payment could be offered which would be conditional upon the good behavior of the vagrant for one year and thus would allow the person to get off scot free. Yet if the person was unable to make such a payment, they would be convicted as a vagrant and fined, imprisoned, or both. When concerning now freed slaves, the laws were much harsher, as many of them, once convicted, were apprenticed to their former owners under a contract or being leased to a corporation. In the contract, the owner was to feed, clothe, and instruct the freed slave in reading, writing, and arithmetic, and, upon the end of the apprenticeship, they were to be given money, a new set of clothes, and a new Bible as payment for the work done. However, such repayment rarely occurred or was enforced by the state government.

Overall in the South, vagrancy laws were so vaguely defined that any free black that was not under the protection of a white person could be arrested. Such laws allowed for police to "round up idle blacks in times of labor scarcity and also gave employers a coercive tool that might be used to keep workers on the job."

With the judicial system having established a means to ensure a continuous supply of cheap labor, the leasing could now begin.

8

Convict Leasing

The act of leasing out convicts isn't anything new, as in states such as Alabama, where the government had no interest in caring for convicts, prisoners were leased out to companies. While this may have helped prisons get convicts off their hands, they made no extra revenue from it. After the Civil War, such leasing began to pick up steam as corporations had access to almost free labor.

Labor scarcity between states was a major problem, and thus concerted efforts were made by each state to keep black prison labor within their borders. This was done be waging war on emigrant agents, people who specialized in moving labor from where it was abundant to where it was scarce. They had done this when slavery was still existent, and it continued under the newly freed slaves. Such agents were viewed as a threat to white farmers, as, by moving black labor here and there, it threatened the establishment of a stable labor source. Though in the early months emigrant agents were ignored, many states established anti-emigrant agent laws due to their need to keep in black labor. One example is in 1876 when Georgia, "Hard hit by black movement to the West," passed legislation that "levied an annual tax of $100 for each county in which a recruiter sought labor. A year later she raised the amount to $500."

Convict leasing, interestingly enough, resulted in power being taken from the state level and given to those at the local level to the point that sheriffs became quite powerful soon after the Civil War ended, as "County sheriffs and judges had dabbled with leasing black convicts out to local famers, or to contractors under hire to repair roads and bridges, beginning almost immediately after the Civil War." This economic empowerment of sheriffs created an incentive for them to convict and lock up as many freedmen as possible and keep a steady supply of labor. An entire economy eventually formed around the convict lease system, including a speculative trade system in convict contracts.

The witnesses and public officials who were owed portions of the lease payments earned by convicts received paper receipts—usually called scrips—from the county that could be redeemed only after the convict had generated enough money to pay them off. Rather than wait for the full amount, holders of scrips would sell their notes for cash to speculators at a lower than face amount. In return, the buyers were to receive the full lease payments—profiting handsomely from those convicts who survived, losing money on the short-lived.

While there was much profit to be made in the convict lease system, not everyone was happy with it—namely, white labor.

9

Labor's Reaction to Convict Leasing

─────────────

Just as how white labor was against slavery due to it undermining their struggle for better working conditions, they were also against the convict lease system for the very same reasons. Never did they stop to consider the fact that both worker and freedman were being manipulated by the very same systems that governed them.

Labor's anti-convict leasing sentiments were felt long before the Civil War began. In 1823 in New York City, journeymen cabinet makers conducted a mass meeting to discuss prison-made goods being introduced to the market and how it threatened their trade. In that same year, also in New York City, mechanics petitioned the state legislature to end the use of prison labor.

During the Civil War, labor unions were opposed to the use of convict labor, arguing that it "tended to lower the wages of thousands of laborers, and in some instances has virtually driven certain kinds of labor out of the field" and that "the contractor is seeking cheap labor and cares nothing for the welfare of the prisoner." However it should be noted that unions were not opposed to all convict labor, as they stated that they were fine with prisoners building a state prison. Thus, the labor unions didn't truly care about the brutal, inhumane treatment of convicts but rather whether the convicts were encroaching on their area of employment.

Yet this should not be examined as a separate battle between free labor and convict labor but rather as a continuation of the struggle between the two groups. Once again, the only way white labor's goals could be achieved was with the destruction of most of the convict lease system to protect their own industries.

While convict leasing may have been profitable for a select few and a thorn in the side to many, eventually the system would have to end.

10

The End of Convict Leasing

Due to a mixture of the changes in the economic and social landscape, convict leasing would eventually die out. However, it is important to first note that the economic and social justifications for such a system reinforced each other, as not only was it "an expedient by which Southern states with depleted treasuries could avoid costly expenditures; it was also one of the greatest single sources of personal wealth to some of the South's leading businessmen and politicians." The southern elites benefitted greatly from the system and thus put all their efforts into perpetuating the system for as long as possible.

If one only looks on the surface at the abolition of convict leasing, they may assume that its demise was due to the public indignation that arose against the system, yet this is not the case—far from it. Rather, it involved a combination of race, politics, and economics depending on the state. For example, in Louisiana, convict leasing was abolished due to it being "part of a reform package which had as its purpose the complete triumph of white supremacy in political affairs," whereas in Tennessee, its leaders decided that the demands of fiscal responsibility dictated abolition when the expense of maintaining the militia at convict stockades—a cost incurred by an armed rebellion on the part of free miners who were displaced by convict gangs—proved greater than the income from the leasing contract.

This system was embedded racism, politics, and economics, but it was also just as much embedded in violence and brutality. Men and women were beaten, bloodied, bruised, and valued only so long as they were able to do labor. They were reduced to nothing more than human resources, human tools to do the bidding of and enrich white industrialists and agriculturalists from the North and the South. From the Civil War to World War II, black Americans were re-enslaved under a new system that was no better than the first.

Being only two generations removed from slavery, families in the black community would have had something to pass down and still have today with only a small percent of profits made from free labor and convict leasing. Think about it: every country that America goes to war with receives money, the banks receive bailouts, the automobile company receives bailouts, the rich pay fewer taxes, even foreigners—non-citizens—of the United States have more rights than blacks. How can America do this? If a foreigner gets wrongly treated in America, even a prisoner of war, a diplomat of that individual's home country would contact the government to make sure they receive due process and are not violated under the law. On the other hand, if blacks are mis-treated, there is no one to call or check to make sure our rights are not violated. The African government will not call for us. We are not considered Africans or Americans; we are African Ameri-cans, a race that was an experiment. To this day white people have the ignorance to say, *If you don't like it, leave*; excuse me, sir, we never asked to come, you destroyed what we knew as our land, language and culture. We are like a substitute teacher: we can act and do the same things as whites, but, when it comes down to it, we are not white—just living the best we can, still surviving 150 years later. If you are an African American, depending on how old you are, people in your family, such as your great-great grandfa-ther, or grandmother, or father or mother if you are over 90 years old, suffered through these conditions.

Let's proceed. Despite seeing an unprecedented degree of black participation in American political life, Reconstruction was ulti-mately frustrating for African Americans, and the rebirth of white supremacy—including the rise of racist organizations such as the Ku Klux Klan—had triumphed in the South by 1877. Almost a century later, resistance to the lingering racism and dis-crimination in America that began during the slavery era would lead to the civil rights movement of the 1960s, which would achieve the greatest political and social gains for blacks since Reconstruction.

11

Civil Rights and Segregation

Blacks made due the best they could from the late 1800s to the early 1900s. There was extreme racism and prejudice, as whites questioned whether it was a good idea for us to be free. Although free from slavery, we still were unable to vote, get loans, and enjoy simple freedoms without being reminded that we are not equal to whites.

African Americans were faced with an almost insurmountable number of obstacles in the 1900s. Moreover, as far as education is concerned, African Americans are given almost no avenue of education K-12, which makes it difficult for them to aspire to higher education, because they don't have the rudiments to get to that point. Public schools are open to African Americans only in very small communities. This is all a tragic carryover from the 1900s.

Laws were made so that socially, politically, economically, and educationally, African Americans were kept out of society. They had to scratch and bite to get whatever advantages that they did get, and the majority could not get those advantages. Look at education, for instance, in 1900 and take, for example, Mississippi, which is a state that spent about three dollars a year on the education of a black child and sixty on the education of a white child; if you look at the whole economic structure in the states of the South that were primarily cotton states and dependent on a sharecropping and the crop lien system for the production of and the profit from this cotton, for which African Americans were the main labor force, black children were forced to work rather than go to school. So even if there was money in the family for shoes and clothing, which often there was not, the children were needed in the labor force. So that was a constraint on African Americans. Politically, African Americans had, for the most part, lost whatever political situation they had had as a result of Reconstruction, and this was done very brutally and systematically. First, it was done outside the law; it was done extra-legally through terrorism, through creating various kinds of laws, and informal ways of keeping African Americans from voting. But by the 1890s all the way up past 1900, such oppression became legal, because various states had formed new constitutional conventions that legally disenfranchised African Americans. So, the political process was closed to them. And then of course later the striking down of the civil rights act meant that all the gains that had been achieved in terms of equality and public accommodations, all of that was dead. So everywhere we looked as a people, the doors seemed to be closed to us.

12

Restrictions on Voting

By 1900, the doors to voting and having a voice in the electoral process had shut down for African Americans. This, after a period during Reconstruction and afterwards of African Americans having a voice, especially and more important for them, a local voice in the way business was conducted in their communities, such as being on juries, having black prosecutors, having black sheriffs, and having black school superintendents. These were the things that were important to African Americans, and this is where they had been able to assert themselves in the electoral process. By the 1880s, when African Americans and poor whites looked like they might form a coalition in the South against the large southern interests, there was a surge of extreme racism and then the converging of what becomes the "solid South." And, as a result of this, as poor whites and wealthy whites began to unite in the late 1880s against African Americans, they began to shut African Americans out. And this was done extra legally. In South Carolina for instance, to keep African Americans from voting, they developed what was called an eight-box law, which meant that for every office you had to put your ballot in the correct box for that office, and if you didn't, then your ballot was invalid. All kinds of means of obstruction were devised. In some of the other states, there was a poll tax whereby if you didn't make a certain amount of money and couldn't pay that tax, then you could not vote. However, they would waive it for white people who were equally poor. So in these extralegal ways, African Americans were kept out of the electoral process. And terrorism, of course, was rampant. But in spite of the terrorism, African Americans continued to try to assert themselves politically, because they recognized how important it was at the local level. By the 1890s, the state governments had decided that they had to make the disenfranchisement of African Americans legal. They began to call state constitutional conventions that developed ways of getting around the 14th and 15th amendments and disenfranchise African Americans completely. So African Americans move from a period in which they actually had a voice in southern government to a situation where they had no say so whatsoever. In addition, the violence did not stop. It's as though the South said, *Okay we're going to disenfranchise you legally, but we're going to make sure that you understand that you cannot rear your head and assert yourself. We have complete hegemony over you, politically, socially and economically.* And brutality was a way of solidifying that stance.

13

Violence

To make sure that African Americans did not attempt to assert themselves in any way, whether it was voting, trying to buy land, and so on, the white South resorted to terrorism. And that terrorism, which was a legacy that never stopped from the time of the Civil War all the way up through this period, reached its fullest intensity in the 1890s and in 1900. It consisted of whipping African Americans, lynching African Americans, and burning African Americans. It consisted of all kinds of violence against African Americans for asserting themselves in any way. And that's what terrorism is about. It's about keeping people from doing something that you think they may want to do. So it wasn't just enough to close these avenues to African Americans; it was designed to say to them *You can't do it, and so don't even try*. But terrorism was very much a part of the legacy of the South and it's something African Americans had lived with. They had periods in which it was not as bad as others. And one of the periods in which it was most intense was during the period of the constitutional convention. Indeed, in the last 16 years of the 19th century, there were 2,500 lynchings in the South. And the majority of them were African Americans.

14

Segregation

By 1900, the South was what we call "Jim Crowed," meaning it was segregated. It hadn't always been that way after the Civil War. Laws were passed that made it illegal to segregate public accommodations, to segregate people on the basis of race in restaurants and theatres, on trains, and so on. Yet, what was the case du jour was not always the case de facto. In spite of the fact that these laws against segregation were there, it didn't mean that they were always obeyed. So, African Americans at any point might be confronted about sitting in a white section. But such confrontation was against the law, and African Americans felt relatively comfortable, especially in urban centers, sitting in places that were integrated. But by the late 1880s segregation became one of the ways in which whites tried to control African Americans, and whites began to become very, very strongly attached to segregated seating, to segregated railroad cars, etc. They used this to separate the races, of course, based on their conception of blacks being inferior. Based especially on the idea that African American men were trying to get close to white women, it was viewed as necessary to create these separate spaces. This began in the late 1880s and escalated along with the other social, political, and economic issues. Segregation became something that was a fact, even if it wasn't a law. Again, like the disenfranchisement movement, it didn't become law until various states began to form new constitutions and put these laws in the new state governments.

By 1900, the majority of the states in the South had called constitutional conventions that legalized segregation. By 1900, in spite of the fact that some states had not done this legally, they had all done it in terms of a fact of life. So, the South was segregated by 1900, and African Americans knew that.

We live in a republic. And in a republic, the laws are based on liberty and on equality. African Americans of that period were not treated like second-class citizens, we were treated as non-citizens. And that's what segregation meant to us. Segregation meant that we had no rights. Segregation meant that we were not going to be seated next to other citizens, that we couldn't use the same facilities as other citizens. So, we were essentially non-citizens. This was a terrible burden for African Americans as a people. And it was something that made many African Americans want to leave the South.

15

Jim Crow Laws

From the 1880s into the 1960s, a majority of American states enforced segregation through "Jim Crow" laws (so called after a black character in minstrel shows). From Delaware to California, and from North Dakota to Texas, many states (and cities, too) could impose legal punishments on people for consorting with members of another race. The most common types of laws forbade intermarriage and ordered business owners and public institutions to keep their black and white clientele separated. Following is a sampling of laws from various states.

Nurses: No person or corporation shall require any white female nurse to nurse in wards or rooms in hospitals, either public or private, in which negro men are placed. Alabama

Buses: All passenger stations in this state operated by any motor transportation company shall have separate waiting rooms or space and separate ticket windows for the white and colored races. Alabama

Railroads: The conductor of each passenger train is authorized and required to assign each passenger to the car or the division of the car, when it is divided by a partition, designated for the race to which such passenger belongs. Alabama

Restaurants: It shall be unlawful to conduct a restaurant or other place for the serving of food in the city, at which white and colored people are served in the same room, unless such white and colored persons are effectually separated by a solid partition extending from the floor upward to a distance of seven feet or higher, and unless a separate entrance from the street is provided for each compartment. Alabama

Pool and Billiard Rooms: It shall be unlawful for a negro and white person to play together or in company with each other at any game of pool or billiards. Alabama

Toilet Facilities, Male: Every employer of white or negro males shall provide for such white or negro males reasonably accessible and separate toilet facilities. Alabama

Intermarriage: The marriage of a person of Caucasian blood with a Negro, Mongolian, Malay, or Hindu shall be null and void. Arizona

Intermarriage: All marriages between a white person and a negro, or between a white person and a person of negro descent to the fourth generation inclusive, are hereby forever prohibited. Florida

Cohabitation: Any negro man and white woman, or any white man and negro woman, who are not married to each other, who shall habitually live in and occupy in the nighttime the same room shall each be punished by imprisonment not exceeding twelve (12) months, or by fine not exceeding five hundred ($500.00) dollars. Florida

Education: The schools for white children and the schools for negro children shall be conducted separately. Florida

Juvenile Delinquents: There shall be separate buildings, not nearer than one fourth mile to each other, one for white boys and one for negro boys. White boys and negro boys shall not, in any manner, be associated together or worked together. Florida

Mental Hospitals: The Board of Control shall see that proper and distinct apartments are arranged for said patients, so that in no case shall Negroes and white persons be together. Georgia

Intermarriage: It shall be unlawful for a white person to marry anyone except a white person. Any marriage in violation of this section shall be void. Georgia

Barbers: No colored barber shall serve as a barber [to] white women or girls. Georgia

Burial: The officer in charge shall not bury, or allow to be buried, any colored persons upon ground set apart or used for the burial of white persons. Georgia

Restaurants: All persons licensed to conduct a restaurant, shall serve either white people exclusively or colored people exclusively and shall not sell to the two races within the same room or serve the two races anywhere under the same license. Georgia

Amateur Baseball: It shall be unlawful for any amateur white baseball team to play baseball on any vacant lot or baseball diamond within two blocks of a playground devoted to the Negro race, and it shall be unlawful for any amateur colored baseball team to play baseball in any vacant lot or baseball diamond within two blocks of any playground devoted to the white race. Georgia

Parks: It shall be unlawful for colored people to frequent any park owned or maintained by the city for the benefit, use and enjoyment of white persons...and unlawful for any white person to frequent any park owned or maintained by the city for the use and benefit of colored persons. Georgia

Wine and Beer: All persons licensed to conduct the business of selling beer or wine...shall serve either white people exclusively or colored people exclusively and shall not sell to the two races within the same room at any time. Georgia

Reform Schools: The children of white and colored races committed to the houses of reform shall be kept entirely separate from each other. Kentucky

Circus Tickets: All circuses, shows, and tent exhibitions, to which the attendance of...more than one race is invited or expected to attend shall provide for the convenience of its patrons not less than two ticket offices with individual ticket sellers, and not less than two entrances to the said performance, with individual ticket takers and receivers, and in the case of outside or tent performances, the said ticket offices shall not be less than twenty-five (25) feet apart. Louisiana

Housing: Any person...who shall rent any part of any such building to a negro person or a negro family when such building is already in whole or in part in occupancy by a white person or white family, or vice versa when the building is in occupancy by a negro person or negro family, shall be guilty of a misdemeanor and on conviction thereof shall be punished by a fine of not less than twenty-five ($25.00) nor more than one hundred ($100.00) dollars or be imprisoned not less than 10, or more than 60 days, or both such fine and imprisonment in the discretion of the court. Louisiana

The Blind: The board of trustees shall...maintain a separate building...on separate ground for the admission, care, instruction, and support of all blind persons of the colored or black race. Louisiana

Intermarriage: All marriages between a white person and a negro, or between a white person and a person of negro descent, to the third generation, inclusive, or between a white person and a member of the Malay race; or between the negro and a member of the Malay race; or between a person of Negro descent, to the third generation, inclusive, and a member of the Malay race, are forever prohibited, and shall be void. Maryland

Railroads: All railroad companies and corporations, and all persons running or operating cars or coaches by steam on any railroad line or track in the State of Maryland, for the transportation of passengers, are hereby required to provide separate cars or coaches for the travel and transportation of the white and colored passengers. Maryland

Education: Separate schools shall be maintained for the children of the white and colored races. Mississippi

Promotion of Equality: Any person...who shall be guilty of printing, publishing or circulating printed, typewritten or written matter urging or presenting for public acceptance or general information, arguments or suggestions in favor of social equality or of intermarriage between whites and negroes, shall be guilty of a misdemeanor and subject to fine or not exceeding five hundred (500.00) dollars or imprisonment not exceeding six (6) months or both. Mississippi

Intermarriage: The marriage of a white person with a negro or mulatto or person who shall have one-eighth or more of negro blood, shall be unlawful and void. Mississippi

Hospital Entrances: There shall be maintained by the governing authorities of every hospital maintained by the state for treatment of white and colored patients separate entrances for white and colored patients and visitors, and such entrances shall be used by the race only for which they are prepared. Mississippi

Prisons: The warden shall see that the white convicts shall have separate apartments for both eating and sleeping from the negro convicts. Mississippi

Education: Separate free schools shall be established for the education of children of African descent; and it shall be unlawful for any colored child to attend any white school, or any white child to attend a colored school. Missouri

Intermarriage: All marriages between...white persons and negroes or white persons and Mongolians...are prohibited and declared absolutely void...No person having one-eighth part or more of negro blood shall be permitted to marry any white person, nor shall any white person be permitted to marry any negro or person having one-eighth part or more of negro blood. Missouri

Education: Separate rooms [shall] be provided for the teaching of pupils of African descent, and [when] said rooms are so provided, such pupils may not be admitted to the school rooms occupied and used by pupils of Caucasian or other descent. New Mexico

Textbooks: Books shall not be interchangeable between the white and colored schools, but shall continue to be used by the race first using them. North Carolina

Libraries: The state librarian is directed to fit up and maintain a separate place for the use of the colored people who may come to the library for the purpose of reading books or periodicals. North Carolina

Militia: The white and colored militia shall be separately enrolled, and shall never be compelled to serve in the same organization. No organization of colored troops shall be permitted where white troops are available, and while white permitted to be organized, colored troops shall be under the command of white officers. North Carolina

Transportation: The...Utilities Commission...is empowered and directed to require the establishment of separate waiting rooms at all stations for the white and colored races. North Carolina

Teaching: Any instructor who shall teach in any school, college or institution where members of the white and colored race are received and enrolled as pupils for instruction shall be deemed guilty of a misdemeanor, and upon conviction thereof, shall be fined in any sum not less than ten dollars ($10.00) nor more than fifty dollars ($50.00) for each offense. Oklahoma

Fishing, Boating, and Bathing: The [Conservation] Commission shall have the right to make segregation of the white and colored races as to the exercise of rights of fishing, boating and bathing. Oklahoma

Mining: The baths and lockers for the negroes shall be separate from the white race, but may be in the same building. Oklahoma

Telephone Booths: The Corporation Commission is hereby vested with power and authority to require telephone companies...to maintain separate booths for white and colored patrons when there is a demand for such separate booths. That the Corporation Commission shall determine the necessity for said separate booths only upon complaint of the people in the town and vicinity to be served after due hearing as now provided by law in other complaints filed with the Corporation Commission. Oklahoma

Lunch Counters: No persons, firms, or corporations, who or which furnish meals to passengers at station restaurants or station eating houses, in times limited by common carriers of said passengers, shall furnish said meals to white and colored passengers in the same room, or at the same table, or at the same counter. South Carolina

Child Custody: It shall be unlawful for any parent, relative, or other white person in this State, having the control or custody of any white child, by right of guardianship, natural or acquired, or otherwise, to dispose of, give or surrender such white child permanently into the custody, control, maintenance, or support, of a negro. South Carolina

Libraries: Any white person of such county may use the county free library under the rules and regulations prescribed by the commissioners court and may be entitled to all the privileges thereof. Said court shall make proper provision for the negroes of said county to be served through a separate branch or branches of the county free library, which shall be administered by [a] custodian of the negro race under the supervision of the county librarian. Texas

Education: [The County Board of Education] shall provide schools of two kinds: those for white children and those for colored children. Texas

Theaters: Every person...operating...any public hall, theatre, opera house, motion picture show or any place of public entertainment or public assemblage which is attended by both white and colored persons, shall separate the white race and the colored race and shall set apart and designate...certain seats therein to be occupied by white persons and a portion thereof , or certain seats therein, to be occupied by colored persons. Virginia

Railroads: The conductors or managers on all such railroads shall have power, and are hereby required, to assign to each white or colored passenger his or her respective car, coach or compartment. If the passenger fails to disclose his race, the conductor and managers, acting in good faith, shall be the sole judges of his race. Virginia

Intermarriage: All marriages of white persons with Negroes, Mulattos, Mongolians, or Malaya hereafter contracted in the State of Wyoming are and shall be illegal and void. Wyoming

Nearly 100 years after the Emancipation Proclamation, African Americans in southern states still inhabited a starkly unequal world of disenfranchisement, segregation, and various forms of oppression, including race-inspired violence. "Jim Crow" laws at the local and state levels barred them from classrooms and bathrooms, from theaters and train cars, from juries and legislatures. In 1954, the U.S. Supreme Court struck down the "separate but equal" doctrine that formed the basis for state-sanctioned discrimination, drawing national and international attention to African Americans' plight. In the turbulent decade and a half that followed, civil rights activists used nonviolent protest and civil disobedience to bring about change, and the federal government made legislative headway with initiatives such as the Voting Rights Act of 1965 and the Civil Rights Act of 1968. Many leaders from within the African American community and beyond rose to prominence during the civil rights era, including Martin Luther King, Jr., Rosa Parks, Malcolm X, Andrew Goodman, and others. They risked—and sometimes lost—their lives in the name of freedom and equality.

Because large segments of the populace—particularly African-Americans, women, and men without property—have not always been accorded full citizenship rights in the American Republic, civil rights movements, or "freedom struggles," have been a frequent feature of the nation's history. In particular, movements to obtain civil rights for black Americans have had special historical significance. Such movements have not only secured citizenship rights for blacks but have also redefined prevailing conceptions of the nature of civil rights and the role of government in protecting these rights. The most important achievements of African American civil rights movements have been the post-Civil War constitutional amendments that abolished slavery and established the citizenship status of blacks and the judicial decisions and legislation based on these amendments, notably the Supreme Court's Brown v. Board of Education of Topeka decision of 1954, the Civil Rights Act of 1964, and the Voting rights Act of 1965. Moreover, these legal changes greatly affected the opportunities available to women, non-black minorities, disabled individuals, and other victims of discrimination.

The modern period of civil rights reform can be divided into several phases, each beginning with isolated, small-scale protests and ultimately resulting in the emergence of new, more militant movements, leaders, and organizations. The Brown decision demonstrated that the litigation strategy of the National Association for the Advancement of Colored People (NAACP) could undermine the legal foundations of southern segregationist practices, but the strategy worked only when blacks, acting individually or in small groups, assumed the risks associated with crossing racial barriers. Thus, even after the Supreme Court declared that public school segregation was unconstitutional, black activism was necessary to compel the federal government to implement the decision and extend its principles to all areas of public life rather than simply in schools. During the 1950s and 1960s, therefore, NAACP-sponsored legal suits and legislative lobbying were supplemented by an increasingly massive and militant social movement seeking a broad range of social changes.

16

Montgomery Bus Boycott and the Southern Christian Leadership Conference

————————

The initial phase of the black protest activity in the post-*Brown* period began on December 1, 1955. Rosa Parks of Montgomery, Alabama, refused to give up her seat to a white bus rider, thereby defying a southern custom that required blacks to give seats toward the front of buses to whites. When she was jailed, a black community boycott of the city's buses began. The boycott lasted more than a year, demonstrating the unity and determination of black residents and inspiring blacks elsewhere.

Martin Luther King, Jr., who emerged as the boycott movement's most effective leader, possessed unique conciliatory and oratorical skills. He understood the larger significance of the boycott and quickly realized that the nonviolent tactics used by the Indian nationalist Mahatma Gandhi could be used by southern blacks. "I had come to see early that the Christian doctrine of love operating through the Ghandhian method of nonviolence was one of the most potent weapons available to the Negro in his struggle for freedom," he explained. Although Parks and King were members of the NAACP, the Montgomery movement led to the creation in 1957 of a new regional organization, the clergy-led Southern Christian Leadership Conference (SCLC), with King as its president.

King remained the major spokesperson for black aspirations, but, as in Montgomery, little-known individuals initiated most subsequent black movements. On February 1, 1960, four freshmen at North Carolina Agricultural and Technical College began a wave of student sit-ins designed to end segregation at southern lunch counters. These protests spread rapidly throughout the South and led to the founding, in April 1960, of the Student Non-Violent Coordinating Committee (SNCC). This student-led group, even more aggressive in its use of nonviolent direct action tactics than King's SCLC, stressed the development of autonomous local movements in contrast to SCLC's strategy of using local campaigns to achieve national civil rights reforms.

17

Birmingham and the March on Washington

The SCLC protest strategy achieved its first major success in 1963 when the group launched a major campaign in Birmingham, Alabama. Highly publicized confrontations between nonviolent protesters, including schoolchildren, on one hand, and police with clubs, fire hoses, and police dogs, on the other, garnered northern attention, sympathetic to the SCLC's cause. The Birmingham clashes and other simultaneous civil rights efforts prompted President John F. Kennedy to push for the passage of new civil rights legislation. By the summer of 1963, the Birmingham protests had become only one of many local protest insurgencies that culminated in the August 28th March on Washington, which attracted at least 200,000 participants. King's address on that occasion captured the idealistic spirit of the expanding protests. "I have a dream," he said, "that one day this nation will rise up and live out the true meaning of its creed—we hold these truths to be self-evident, that all men are created equal."

Although some whites reacted negatively to the spreading protests of 1963, King's linkage of black militancy and idealism helped bring about passage of the Civil Rights Act of 1964. This legislation outlawed segregation in public facilities and racial discrimination in employment and education. In addition to blacks, women and other victims of discrimination benefited from the act.

18

Freedom Summer

While the SCLC focused its efforts in the urban centers, SNCC's activities were concentrated in the rural Black Belt areas of Georgia, Alabama, and Mississippi, where white resistance was intense. Although the NAACP and the predominantly white Congress of Racial Equality (CORE) also contributed activists to the Mississippi movement, young SNCC organizers spearheaded civil rights efforts in the state. Black residents in the Black Belt, many of whom had been involved in civil rights efforts since the 1940s and 1950s, emphasized voter registration rather than desegregation as a goal. Mississippi residents Amzie Moore and Fannie Lou Hamer were among the grassroots leaders who worked closely with the SNCC to build new organizations, such as the Mississippi Freedom Democratic Party (MFDP). Although the MFDP did not succeed in its attempt to claim the seats of the all-white Mississippi delegation at the 1964 National Democratic Convention in Atlantic City, it attracted national attention and thus prepared the way for a major upsurge in southern black political activity.

After the Atlantic City experience, disillusioned SNCC organizers worked with local leaders in Alabama to create the Lowndes County Freedom Organization. The symbol they chose—the Black Panther—reflected the radicalism and a belief in racial separatism that increasingly characterized SNCC during the last half of the 1960s. The black panther symbol was later adopted by the California-based Black Panther Party, formed in 1966 by Huey Newton and Bobby Seale.

19

Selma to Montgomery March

Despite occasional open conflicts between the two groups, both the SCLC's protest strategy and the SNCC's organizing activities were responsible for major Alabama protests in 1965, which prompted President Lyndon B. Johnson to introduce new voting rights legislation. On March 7th, an SCLC-planned march from Selma to the state capitol in Montgomery ended almost before it began at Pettus Bridge on the outskirts of Selma, when mounted police using tear gas and wielding clubs attacked the protesters. News accounts of "Bloody Sunday" brought hundreds of civil rights sympathizers to Selma. Many demonstrators were determined to mobilize another march, and SNCC activists challenged King to defy a court order forbidding such marches. But reluctant to do anything that would lessen public support for the voting rights cause, King on March 9th turned back a second march to the Pettus Bridge when it was blocked by the police. That evening a group of Selma whites killed a northern white minister who had joined the demonstrations. In contrast to the killing of a black man, Jimmy Lee Jackson, a few weeks before, the Reverend James Reeb's death led to a national outcry. After several postponements of the march, civil rights advocates finally gained court permission to proceed. This Selma to Montgomery march was the culmination of a stage of the African American freedom struggle. Soon afterward, Congress passed the Voting Rights Act of 1965, which greatly increased the number of southern blacks able to register to vote. But it was also the last major racial protest of the 1960s to receive substantial white support.

20

Rise of Black Nationalism

By the late 1960s, organizations such as the NAACP, SCLC, and SNCC faced increasingly strong challenges from new militant organizations, such as the Black Panther Party. The Panthers' strategy of "picking up the gun" reflected the sentiments of many inner-city blacks. A series of major "riots" (as the authorities called them), or "rebellions" (the sympathizers' term), erupted during the last half of the 1960s. Often influenced by the black nationalism of Elijah Muhammad and Malcolm X and by pan-African leaders, proponents of black liberation saw civil rights reforms as insufficient, because they did not address the problems faced by millions of poor blacks and because African American citizenship was derived ultimately from the involuntary circumstances of enslavement. In addition, proponents of racial liberation often saw the African American freedom struggle in international terms, as a movement for human rights and national self-determination for all peoples.

21

Post-1960s Civil Rights Movement

Severe government repression, the assassinations of Malcolm X and Martin Luther King, Jr., and the intense infighting within the black militant community caused a decline in protest activity after the 1960s. The African American freedom struggle nevertheless left a permanent mark on American society. Overt forms of racial discrimination and government-supported segregation of public facilities came to an end, although de facto, as opposed to de jure, segregation persisted in northern as well as southern public school systems and in other areas of American society. In the South, anti-black violence declined. Black candidates were elected to political offices in communities where blacks had once been barred from voting, and many of the leaders or organizations that came into existence during the 1950s and 1960s remained active in southern politics. Southern colleges and universities that once excluded blacks began to recruit them.

Despite the civil rights gains of the 1960s, however, racial discrimination and repression remained a significant factor in American life. Even after President Johnson declared a war on poverty and King initiated a Poor People's Campaign in 1968, the distribution of the nation's wealth and income moved toward greater inequality during the 1970s and 1980s. Civil rights advocates acknowledged that desegregation had not brought significant improvements in the lives of poor blacks, but they were divided over the future direction of black advancement efforts. To a large degree, moreover, many of the civil rights efforts of the 1970s and 1980s were devoted to defending previous gains or strengthening enforcement mechanisms.

The modern African American civil rights movement, like similar earlier movements, had transformed American democracy. It also served as a model for other group advancement and group pride efforts involving women, students, Chicanos, gays and lesbians, the elderly, and many others. Continuing controversies regarding affirmative action programs and compensatory remedies for historically rooted patterns of discrimination were aspects of more fundamental, ongoing debates about the boundaries of individual freedom, the role of government, and alternative concepts of social justice.

Against the will of the white government officials, African Americans were making progress by the 1950s, if by nothing else by recognizing that we have a voice, educating ourselves on the laws, and taking small stands against injustice in the South and North. Amidst being separated, punished, withheld from proper education, laws, and equal rights, our leaders were killed. The only president that spoke out for us had been murdered. KKK outrage, hangings, and lynching plagued the land.

22

The Party Starts

In October of 1966, in Oakland, California, Huey Newton and Bobby Seale founded the Black Panther Party for Self-Defense. The Panthers practiced militant self-defense of minority communities against the U.S. Government and fought to establish revolutionary socialism through mass organizing and community-based programs. The party was one of the first organizations in U.S. history to militantly struggle for ethnic minority and working class emancipation—a party whose agenda was the revolutionary establishment of *real* economic, social, and political equality across gender and color lines.

The practices of the late Malcolm X were deeply rooted in the theoretical foundations of the Black Panther Party. Malcolm had represented both a militant revolutionary, with the dignity and self-respect to stand up and fight to win equality for all oppressed minorities, while also being an outstanding role model, someone who sought to bring about positive social services—something the Black Panthers would take to new heights. The Panthers followed Malcolm's belief in international working class unity across the spectrum of color and gender and thus united with various minority and white revolutionary groups. From the tenets of Maoism, they set the role of their party as the vanguard of the revolution and worked to establish a united front, while from Marxism they addressed the capitalist economic system, embraced the theory of dialectical materialism, and represented the need for all workers to forcefully take over the means of production.

On April 25th, 1967, the first issue of *The Black Panther*, the party's official news organ, went into distribution. In the following month, the party marched on the California state capital fully armed, in protest of the state's attempt to outlaw carrying loaded weapons in public. Bobby Seale read a statement of protest, while the police responded by immediately arresting him and all 30 armed Panthers. This early act of political repression kindled the fires of the burning resistance movement in the United States, soon initiating minority workers to take up arms and form new Panther chapters outside the state.

In October of 1967, the police arrest the Defense Minister of the Panthers, Huey Newton, for killing an Oakland cop. Panther Eldridge Cleaver began the movement to "Free Huey," a struggle the Panthers would devote a great deal of their attention to in the coming years, while the party spread its roots further into the political spectrum, forming coalitions with various revolutionary parties. Stokely Carmichael, the former chairman of the Student Nonviolent Coordinating Committee (SNCC) and a nationally known proponent of Black Power, was recruited into the party through this struggle and soon became the party's Prime Minister in February 1968. Carmichael was adamantly against allowing whites into the black liberation movement, explaining that whites cannot relate to the black experience and have an intimidating effect on blacks; a position that stirred opposition within the Panthers. Carmichael explained: "Whites who come into the black community with ideas of change seem to want to absolve the power structure of its responsibility for what it is doing, and say that change can only come through black unity, which is the worst kind of paternalism. If we are to proceed toward true liberation, we must cut ourselves off from white people..... [otherwise] we will find ourselves entwined in the tentacles of the white power complex that controls this country."

At the beginning of 1968, after selling Mao's Red Book to university students in order to buy shotguns, the Party made the book required reading. Meanwhile, the FBI, under J. Edgar Hoover, began a program called COINTELPRO (counterintelligence program) to break up the spreading unity of revolutionary groups that had begun solidifying through the work and example of the Panthers—the Peace and Freedom Party, the Brown Berets, Students for a Democratic Society, the SNCC, the SCLC, the Poor People's March, Cesar Chavez and others in the farm labor movement, the American Indian Movement, the Young Puerto Rican Brothers, the Young Lords, and many others. To destroy the party, the FBI began with a program of surgical assassinations—killing leading members of the party who they knew could not be otherwise subverted. Following these mass killings would be a series of arrests, followed by a program of psychological warfare, designed to split the party both politically and morally through the use of espionage, provocateurs, and chemical warfare.

On April 6, 1968, in West Oakland, Bobby Hutton, 17 years old, was shot dead by Oakland police. In a 90-minute gun battle, an unarmed Bobby Hutton was shot 10 times after his house was set ablaze and he was forced to run out into a fire of bullets. Just two days earlier, Martin Luther King, Jr. was assassinated after he had begun rethinking his own doctrines of nonviolence and started to build ties with radical unions. Two months later, on the day of Bobby's death, Robert Kennedy, widely recognized in the minority community as one of the only politicians in the U.S. "sympathetic" to the civil rights movement, was also assassinated.

In January 1969, the first Panther's Free Breakfast for School Children Program was initiated at St. Augustine's Church in Oakland. By the end of the year, the Panthers had set up kitchens in cities across the nation, feeding over 10,000 children *every day* before they went to school.

A few months later, J. Edgar Hoover publicly stated that the Panthers posed the "greatest threat to the internal security of the country."

In Chicago, the outstanding leader of the Panthers local, Fred Hampton, led five different breakfast programs on the West Side, helped create a free medical center, initiated a door-to-door program of health services that tested for sickle cell anemia, and encouraged blood drives for the Cook County Hospital. The Chicago party also began reaching out to local gangs to clean up their acts, get them away from crime, and bring them into the class war. The Party's efforts met with wide success, and Hampton's audiences and organized contingent grew by the day.

On December 4th, at 4:00 in the morning, thanks to information from an FBI informant, Chicago police raid the Panthers' Chicago apartment, murdering Fred Hampton while he slept in his bed. He was shot twice in the head and once in the arm and shoulder, while three other people *sleeping in the same bed* escaped unharmed. Mark Clark, sleeping in the living room chair, was also murdered while asleep. Hampton's wife, carrying child for 8 months, was also shot but survived. Four Panthers sleeping in the apartment were wounded, while one other escaped injury . Fred Hampton was 21 years old when he was executed, and Mark was 17 years old. According to the findings of the federal grand jury, 90 bullets were fired inside the apartment. One came from a Panther—Mark—who slept with a shotgun in his hand. All surviving Panther members were arrested for "attempted murder of the police and aggravated assault." Not a single cop spent a moment in jail for the executions.

In the summer of 1969, the alliance between the Panthers and the SNCC began ripping apart. One of the main points of dispute was the inclusion of whites in the struggle for minority liberation, a dispute which was pushed into an open gun fight at the University of California in Los Angeles against the group US, led by Maulana Karenga, which left two Panthers dead. In September, in the government's court house, Huey Newton was convicted of voluntary manslaughter and sentenced to 2 to 15 years in prison; by 1970, the conviction was appealed and overturned on procedural errors. On November 24, 1968, Kathleen and Eldridge

Cleaver fled the U.S., visited Cuba and Paris, and eventually settle in Algeria. Earlier in the year Cleaver had published his famous book *Soul on Ice*. By the end of the year, the party had swelled from 400 members to over 5,000 members in 45 chapters and branches, with a newspaper circulation of 100,000 copies.

In 1969 Seale was indicted in Chicago for protesting during the Democratic National Convention of the previous year. The court refused to allow Seale to choose a lawyer. As Seale repeatedly stood up during the show trial insisting that he was being denied his constitutional right to counsel, the judge ordered him bound and gagged. He was convicted on 16 counts of contempt and sentenced to four years in prison. While in jail, he would be charged again for killing a cop in years past, a trial that would end in 1971 with a hung jury.

In March 1970, Bobby Seale published *Seize The Time* while still being held in prison, the story of the Panthers and Huey Newton. On April 2, 1970, in New York, 21 Panthers were charged with plotting to assassinate police officers and blow up buildings. On May 22nd, eight members, including Ericka Huggins, were arrested on a variety of conspiracy and murder charges in New Haven, Connecticut. Meanwhile, Chief of Staff David Hilliard was on trial for threatening President Richard Nixon. The party did little to separate its legal and illegal aspects and was thus always and everywhere under attack by the government. In 1971, the Panther's newspaper circulation reached 250,000.

On Huey Newton's release from prison, he devoted more effort to further developing the Panther's socialist survival programs in black communities—programs that provided free breakfasts for children, established free medical clinics, helped the homeless find housing, and gave away free clothing and food.

In March 1970, the FBI began to sow seeds of factionalism in the Black Panthers, in part by forging letters to members. Eldridge Cleaver was one of their main targets—living in exile in Algiers—they gradually convinced him with a steady stream of misinformation that the Panther Party leadership was trying to remove him from power. Cleaver received stacks of forged FBI letters from supposed party members, criticizing Netwon's leadership and asking for Cleaver to take control. Following is an example of such a forged letter, written using the name of Connie Matthews, Newton's personal secretary:

> I know you have not been told what has been happening lately.... Things around headquarters are dreadfully disorganized with the comrade commander not making proper decisions. The newspaper is in a shambles. No one knows who is in charge. The foreign department gets no support. Brothers and sisters are accused of all sorts of things...
>
> I am disturbed because I, myself, do not know which way to turn.... If only you were here to inject some strength into the movement, or to give some advice. One of two steps must be taken soon and both are drastic. We must either get rid of the supreme commander or get rid of the disloyal members... Huey is really all we have right now, and we can't let him down, regardless of how poorly he is acting, unless you feel otherwise.

Cleaver received similar forged letters across the spectrum, from groups outside the Panthers, to Panthers themselves, from rank and file members to Elbert "Big Man" Howard, editor of the Black Panther. The split came when Newton went onto a T.V. talk show for an interview, with Cleaver on the phone in Algiers. Cleaver expressed his absolute disdain for what had happened to the party, demanded that David Hilliard (Chief of Staff) be removed, and even attacked the breakfast program as reformist. Cleaver was expelled from the Central Committee and started up his own Black Liberation Army. In 1973, Seale ran for mayor of Oakland. Though he received 40% of the vote, he was defeated.

With such great struggles, seeing the party being ripped apart by factions and internal hatred, Huey, like many members, became disillusioned. He no longer wanted to lead the party, though many expected and demanded otherwise, and he spun into a spiral of self-doubt. He became heavily dependent on cocaine, heroin, and other drugs. It was not clear this was his own doing and was very probably the work of the FBI. Huey remarked in one of his public speeches in the 1980s that he would often have spurts of his brilliant clarity but then become entirely incoherent and rambling and that he was killing himself by reactionary suicide through the vices of drug addiction. On August 22, 1989, Newton was shot dead on the streets of Oakland in a drug dispute.

Bobby Seale resigned from the party, and Elaine Brown took the lead in continuing the Panther community programs. In the fall of 1975, Eldridge and Kathleen Cleaver returned from exile as born-again Christians. In 1979, all charges against Cleaver were dropped after he bargained with the state and pled guilty to assault in a 1968 shootout with the cops. He was put on five years' probation. In the dimming years of his life, Cleaver assimilated a political outlook similar to that of Martin Luther King, Jr., engaged in various business ventures, and became heavily addicted to cocaine.

By the beginning of the 1980s, attacks on the party and internal degradation and divisions caused the party to fall apart. The leadership of the party had been absolutely smashed, and its rank and file were constantly terrorized by the police. Many remaining Panthers were hunted down and killed in the following years and imprisoned on trumped charges (Mumia Abu-Jamal and Sundiata Acoli, among many others) or forced to flee the United States (Assata Shakur and others).

As Cleaver would later explain in an interview a year before his death: "As it was [the U.S. government] chopped off the head [of the Black liberation movement] and left the body there armed. That's why all these young bloods are out there now, they've got the rhetoric but are without the political direction... and they've got the guns."

23

Black Child's Pledge

———————

I pledge allegiance to my Black People.

I pledge to develop my mind and body to the greatest extent possible.

I will learn all that I can in order to give my best to my People in their struggle for liberation.

I will keep myself physically fit, building a strong body free from drugs and other substances which weaken me and make me less capable of protecting myself, my family, and my Black brothers and sisters.

I will unselfishly share my knowledge and understanding with them in order to bring about change more quickly.

———

I will discipline myself to direct my energies thoughtfully and constructively rather than wasting them in idle hatred.

I will train myself never to hurt or allow others to harm my Black brothers and sisters, for I recognize that we need every Black Man, Woman, and Child to be physically, mentally, and psychologically strong.

These principles I pledge to practice daily and to teach them to others in order to unite my People.

Panther Ten Point Program October 15, 1966

We Want Freedom. We Want Power to Determine the Destiny of Our Black Community.

We believe that Black people will not be free until we are able to determine our destiny.

We Want Full Employment for Our People.

We believe that the federal government is responsible and obligated to give every man employment or a guaranteed income. We believe that if the White American businessmen will not give full employment, then the means of production should be taken from the businessmen and placed in the community so that the people of the community can organize and employ all of its people and give a high standard of living.

We Want an End to the Robbery by the Capitalists of Our Black Community.

We believe that this racist government has robbed us, and now we are demanding the overdue debt of forty acres and two mules. Forty acres and two mules were promised 100 years ago as restitution for slave labor and mass murder of Black people. We will accept the payment in currency which will be distributed to our many communities. The Germans are now aiding the Jews in Israel for the genocide of the Jewish people. The Germans murdered six million Jews. The American racist has taken part in the slaughter of over fifty million Black people; therefore, we feel that this is a modest demand that we make.

We Want Decent Housing Fit for the Shelter of Human Beings.

We believe that if the White Landlords will not give decent housing to our Black community, then the housing and the land should be made into cooperatives so that our community, with government aid, can build and make decent housing for its people.

We Want Education for Our People that Exposes the True Nature of this Decadent American Society.

We Want Education that Teaches Us Our True History and Our Role in the Present-Day Society.

We believe in an educational system that will give to our people a knowledge of self. If a man does not have knowledge of himself and his position in society and the world, then he has little chance to relate to anything else.

We Want All Black Men to Be Exempt From Military Service.

We believe that Black people should not be forced to fight in the military service to defend a racist government that does not protect us. We will not fight and kill other people of color in the world who, like Black people, are being victimized by the White racist government of America. We will protect ourselves from the force and violence of the racist police and the racist military, by whatever means necessary.

We Want an Immediate End to Police Brutality and Murder of Black People.

We believe we can end police brutality in our Black community by organizing Black self-defense groups that are dedicated to defending our Black community from racist police oppression and brutality. The Second Amendment to the Constitution of the United States gives a right to bear arms. We therefore believe that all Black people should arm themselves for self-defense.

We Want Freedom for All Black Men Held in Federal, State, County, and City Prisons and Jails.

We believe that all Black people should be released from the many jails and prisons, because they have not received a fair and impartial trial.

We Want All Black People When Brought to Trial to Be Tried in Court by a Jury of Their Peer Group or People From their Black Communities, as Defined by the Constitution of the United States.

We believe that the courts should follow the United States

Constitution so that Black people will receive fair trials. The Fourteenth Amendment of the U.S. Constitution gives a man a right to be tried by his peer group. A peer is a person from a similar economic, social, religious, geographical, environmental, historical and racial background. To do this the court will be forced to select a jury from the Black community from which the Black defendant came. We have been, and are being, tried by all-White juries that have no understanding of the "average reasoning man" of the Black community.

We Want Land, Bread, Housing, Education, Clothing, Justice and Peace.

When, in the course of human events, it becomes necessary for one people to dissolve the political bonds which have connected them with another, and to assume, among the powers of the earth, the separate and equal station to which the laws of nature and nature's God entitle them, a decent respect of the opinions of mankind requires that they should declare the causes which impel them to the separation.

We hold these truths to be self-evident, that all men are created equal; that they are endowed by their Creator with certain inalienable rights; that among these are life, liberty, and the pursuit of happiness. That, to secure these rights, governments are instituted among men, deriving their just powers from the consent of the governed; that, whenever any form of government becomes destructive of these ends, it is the right of the people to alter or abolish it, and to institute a new government, laying its foundation on such principles, and organizing its powers in such form, as to them shall seem most likely to effect their safety and happiness. Prudence, indeed, will dictate that governments long established should not be changed for light and transient causes; and, accordingly, all experience hath shown that mankind are more disposed to suffer, while evils are sufferable, than to right themselves by abolishing the forms to which they are accustomed. But, when a long train of abuses and usurpations, pursuing invariably the same object, evinces a design to reduce them under absolute despotism, it is their right, it is their duty, to throw off such government, and to provide new guards for their future security.

24

War on Drugs

Traces from the War on Drugs can be found from President Nixon to the draconian Rockefeller Drug Laws to the emerging aboveground marijuana market that is poised to make legal millions for wealthy investors doing the same thing that generations of people of color have been arrested and locked up for.

The Early Stages

Many currently illegal drugs, such as marijuana, opium, coca, and psychedelics have been used for thousands of years for both medical and spiritual purposes. So why are some drugs legal and other drugs illegal today? It's not based on any scientific assessment of the relative risks of these drugs—but it has everything to do with who is associated with these drugs.

The first anti-opium laws in the 1870s were directed at Chinese immigrants. The first anti-cocaine laws, in the South in the early

1900s, were directed at black men. The first anti-marijuana laws, in the Midwest and the Southwest in the 1910s and 20s, were directed at Mexican migrants and Mexican Americans. Today, Latino and especially black communities are still subject to wildly disproportionate drug enforcement and sentencing practices.

Nixon

In the 1960s, as drugs became symbols of youthful rebellion, social upheaval, and political dissent, the government halted scientific research to evaluate their medical safety and efficacy. In June 1971, President Nixon declared a "war on drugs." He dramatically increased the size and presence of federal drug control agencies and pushed through measures such as mandatory sentencing and no-knock warrants. Nixon temporarily placed marijuana in Schedule One, the most restrictive category of drugs, pending review by a commission he appointed led by Republican Pennsylvania Governor Raymond Shafer.

In 1972, the commission unanimously recommended decriminalizing the possession and distribution of marijuana for personal use. Nixon ignored the report and rejected its recommendations.

Between 1973 and 1977, however, 11 states decriminalized marijuana possession. In January 1977, President Jimmy Carter was inaugurated on a campaign platform that included marijuana decriminalization. In October 1977, the Senate Judiciary Committee voted to decriminalize possession of up to an ounce of marijuana for personal use.

Within just a few years, though, the tide had shifted. Proposals to decriminalize marijuana were abandoned as parents became increasingly concerned about high rates of teen marijuana use. Marijuana was ultimately caught up in a broader cultural backlash against the perceived permissiveness of the 1970s.

The presidency of Ronald Reagan marked the start of a long period of skyrocketing rates of incarceration, largely thanks to his unprecedented expansion of the drug war. The number of people behind bars for nonviolent drug law offenses increased from 50,000 in 1980 to over 400,000 by 1997.

Public concern about illicit drug use built throughout the 1980s, largely due to media portrayals of people addicted to the smokeable form of cocaine dubbed "crack." Soon after Ronald Reagan took office in 1981, his wife, Nancy Reagan, began a highly publicized anti-drug campaign, coining the slogan "Just Say No."

This set the stage for the zero tolerance policies implemented in the mid-to-late 1980s. Los Angeles Police Chief Daryl Gates, who believed that "casual drug users should be taken out and shot," founded the DARE drug education program, which was quickly adopted nationwide despite the lack of evidence of its effectiveness. The increasingly harsh drug policies also blocked the expansion of syringe access programs and other harm reduction policies to reduce the rapid spread of HIV/AIDS.

In the late 1980s, a political hysteria about drugs led to the passage of draconian penalties in Congress and state legislatures that rapidly increased the prison population. In 1985, the proportion of Americans polled who saw drug abuse as the nation's "number one problem" was just 2–6%. The figure grew through the remainder of the 1980s until, in September 1989, it reached a remarkable 64%—one of the most intense fixations by the American public on any issue in polling history. Within less than a year, however, the figure plummeted to less than 10% as the media lost interest. The draconian policies enacted during the hysteria remained, however, and continued to result in escalating levels of arrests and incarceration.

Although Bill Clinton advocated for treatment instead of incarceration during his 1992 presidential campaign, after his first few months in the White House he reverted to the strategies of his Republican predecessors by continuing to escalate the drug war. Notoriously, Clinton rejected a U.S. Sentencing Commission recommendation to eliminate the disparity between crack and powder cocaine sentences.

He also rejected, with the encouragement of drug czar General Barry McCaffrey, health secretary Donna Shalala's advice to end the federal ban on funding for syringe access programs. Yet, a month before leaving office, Clinton asserted in a Rolling Stone interview that "we really need a re-examination of our entire policy on imprisonment" of people who use drugs and said that marijuana use "should be decriminalized."

At the height of the drug war hysteria in the late 1980s and early 1990s, a movement emerged seeking a new approach to drug policy. In 1987, Arnold Trebach and Kevin Zeese founded the Drug Policy Foundation—describing it as the "loyal opposition to the war on drugs." Prominent conservatives such as William Buckley and Milton Friedman had long advocated for ending drug prohibition, as had civil libertarians such as longtime ACLU Executive

Director Ira Glasser. In the late 1980s, they were joined by Baltimore Mayor Kurt Schmoke, Federal Judge Robert Sweet, Princeton professor Ethan Nadelmann, and other activists, scholars, and policymakers.

In 1994, Nadelmann founded The Lindesmith Center as the first U.S. project of George Soros's Open Society Institute. In 2000, the growing Center merged with the Drug Policy Foundation to create the Drug Policy Alliance.

George W. Bush arrived in the White House as the drug war was running out of steam—yet he allocated more money than ever to it. His drug czar, John Walters, zealously focused on marijuana and launched a major campaign to promote student drug testing. While rates of illicit drug use remained constant, overdose fatalities rose rapidly.

The era of George W. Bush also witnessed the rapid escalation of the militarization of domestic drug law enforcement. By the end of Bush's term, there were about 40,000 paramilitary-style SWAT raids on Americans every year—mostly for nonviolent drug law offenses, often misdemeanors. While federal reform mostly stalled under Bush, state-level reforms finally began to slow the growth of the drug war.

Politicians now routinely admit to having used marijuana, and even cocaine, when they were younger. When Michael Bloomberg was questioned during his 2001 mayoral campaign about whether he had ever used marijuana, he said, "You bet I did—and I enjoyed it." Barack Obama also candidly discussed his prior cocaine and marijuana use: "When I was a kid, I inhaled frequently—that was the point."

The assault on American citizens, however, has persisted. President Obama, despite advocating for reforms—such as reducing the crack/powder sentencing disparity, ending the ban on federal funding for syringe access programs, and supporting state medical marijuana laws—has yet to shift the majority of drug control funding to a health-based approach.

Marijuana reform has gained unprecedented momentum throughout the Americas. Colorado, Washington, Alaska, Oregon, and Washington D.C. have legalized marijuana for adults. In December 2013, Uruguay became the first country in the world to legally regulate marijuana. In Canada, Prime Minister Justin Trudeau has promise to legalize marijuana.

Public opinion has shifted dramatically in favor of sensible reforms that expand health-based approaches while reducing the role of criminalization in drug policy. Yet the assault on American citizens and others continues, with 700,000 people still arrested for marijuana offenses each year and almost 500,000 people still behind bars for nothing more than a drug law violation.

Progress is inevitably slow, but there is unprecedented momentum behind drug policy reform right now. We look forward to a future where drug policies are shaped by science and compassion rather than political hysteria.

The war on drugs was just another name for a war on blacks. The government continues to push large quantities of drugs, and guns, into largely black-populated areas and arrest blacks and issue lengthy sentences for nonviolent crimes. This has been going on for over 30 years and has destroyed millions of black families. Blacks are not forced to participate in illegal activity, but when your conditions are incredibly poor and you have to feed your family, and there is a way you can make easy money, your choices are limited. You turn to a life of crime—sounds similar to the slaves when they were freed, correct? Yes, it is exactly the same. The question to ask is still, *where are the sentences for the people who are producing the drugs, guns, and ammunition and smuggling it into inner-city communities at an alarming rate?* Furthermore, blacks who get convicted of the exact same charges as whites receive a 5–7 times longer sentence. Seem familiar again? Recall convict leasing.

White privilege (or **white skin privilege**) is a term for societal privileges that benefit people identified as white in Western countries, beyond what is commonly experienced by non-white people under the same social, political, or economic circumstances. Academic perspectives such as critical race theory and whiteness studies use the concept of "white privilege" to analyze how racism and racialized societies affect the lives of white or white-skinned people.

There is an expression "You don't get a second chance to make a first impression"; white people's first impression of blacks was that of a barbaric people, who lives were of no value, an inferior race. When you go into a job interview, you can be dressed in the same suit as your white counterpart, but because you have a black face, you are categorized; they have an impression of you even before you speak one word. This is not your fault, or their fault, it is history's fault. There will always be an underlying layer of supremacy, or guilt, by whites and revenge or dominance, or inferiority, by blacks. All this without one spoken word.

25

Public Housing

Public housing is a program introduced at the federal level in 1937 that provides for public financing of low-cost housing in the form of publicly managed and owned multi-family developments. Several municipalities, most notably New York City, had started to provide publicly funded housing prior to the introduction of the 1937 Housing Act, and it was these kinds of programs that became the model for the federal program. Public housing was not originally built to house the "poorest of the poor" but rather was intended for select segments of the working class. Specifically, it was designed to serve the needs of the "submerged middle class," who were temporarily outside of the labor market during the Great Depression. After World War II, many working class people were able to buy their own homes using low-interest mortgages through the VA and FHA. These benefits were targeted to whites and helped move whites to suburbs but kept blacks concentrated in cities and inner suburbs (especially in the northeastern and mid-western states). The distribution of federal benefits made it possible for mostly white working-class people to move out of public housing and contributed to a downward income shift in the public housing population after the 1940s. The discriminatory nature of these practices has been well documented. Public housing has also been thought of as a solution for inner-city poverty and isolation and as a basic human necessity for less well-off people (blacks). The view of many planners, architects, and social workers was that good housing was humane and necessary for the well-being of all people and would greatly improve life chances for slum dwellers. They saw public housing as way of fulfilling part of the state's responsibility to ensure that decent, affordable housing was available for all residents of the U.S. Early reformers were appalled by the conditions in the tenements where immigrants lived. They called for the demolition of the tenements, an end to windowless interior rooms, better air circulation, and more light. They ascribed many of the undesirable qualities of the poor to their unsafe and unsanitary living conditions. By the turn of the century, housing commissions had been set up in several major cities in order to impose some regulations on landlords. The first national housing legislation was passed in 1937 after a long struggle in Congress. Beyond providing low-cost housing, the other purpose behind the original 1937 legislation was to improve the lagging economy by providing jobs in the building industry. Indeed, public housing was never conceived of as providing long-term permanent housing for the poor. The explicit purpose of the act was "...to alleviate present and recurring unemployment and to remedy the unsafe and insanitary housing conditions and the acute shortage of decent, safe and sanitary dwellings for families of low income." The addition of the "alleviation of unemployment" as one of the purposes of the act was a way in which the original legislation was modified in order to be accepted by Congress. The act also provided for slum clearance and the provision of replacement "low-rent housing."

This housing was to be consumed by "families of low income," which had a rather loose definition as "...families...in the lowest income group who cannot afford to pay enough to cause private enterprise...to build an adequate supply of decent, safe, and sanitary dwellings." The only directive for the income screening of tenants was that their incomes be no higher than five times the rental cost of the unit (six times in the case of families with three or more children). Some of the earliest advocates of public housing supported tenant screening, because they knew that to have a successful housing development most residents must be employed. Qualitative tenant screening was the norm when public housing was first built in the late 1930s. These practices were challenged in the 1960s, but there was a paradoxical criticism of the way public housing was managed; on one hand, some managers were criticized for the laxity of rules, while others were maligned for being too strict and moralistic, demonstrating the inconsistent standards by which public housing was judged . In the 1950s and earlier, very strict tenant policies were enforced. Unwed pregnant women could be evicted, and large fines for property damage were imposed. Other criteria were that families have two parents, the head of the household holds a job, and that families have some record of good housekeeping skills. In fact, visits were made to future tenants' previous dwellings to see if they were suitable candidates. It was also common to make spot checks in public housing developments to make sure units were being well cared for. Even into the second and third decades of public housing, spot checks to catch extra tenants (especially men living with unmarried welfare recipients) were not infrequent and continue in some places. In the 1940s and 1950s, income limits had the effect of penalizing residents for upward mobility. Families could be evicted if their income surpassed an upper limit. The Housing Act of 1949 introduced subsidized housing programs other than public housing and included a housing priority for very low-income people, income limits, and maximum rents (rents were required to be 20% less than the lowest market rates. This benefited business interests by limiting the program to the very poor and leaving the working class to be housed by private builders. Limiting the program in this way ensured non-competitiveness with the private sector and was not motivated by a desire to serve the most needy in society. In the late 1960s, further incentives were introduced to encourage the involvement of private developers and real estate interests in the development of low-cost housing in the form of public financing of private subsidized housing developments. These programs gave private developers tax breaks, low-cost mortgages, and rent subsidies to house the poor. This marked the beginning of corrupt practices in the administration of some housing subsidy programs that led to the HUD scandals of the 1970s, which were visited again in the 1980s. While the public housing program was not directly implicated in the abuses, the problems weakened support for all federal housing programs. Despite problems in the implementation of housing subsidy programs, the direction of housing policy was steadily moving away from supply-based models and towards subsidized private development and demand-based delivery systems, such as housing vouchers. Ironically, while ending legal discrimination by no longer allowing racially segregated projects, the Civil Rights Act of 1964 contributed to the movement of whites out of projects when they became racially integrated. Over time, advocates for the poor asked that preferences on waiting lists be given to the most disadvantaged applicants, in particular to the homeless and displaced. This, combined with income limits, ensured that public housing residents were drawn from the least well-off segments of society. Anyone who could afford to live elsewhere moved out of public housing, and whites had more opportunities than minorities to take advantage of government subsidies that promoted homeownership. In 1981, rent ceilings were eliminated, which potentially made public housing even less attractive to its higher-income residents. Additionally, the proportion of tenants with incomes over 50% of median was limited. Rents were changed to reflect a payment of 30% of adjusted income, an increase from 25%. Discretion as to how to calculate standard deductions from total income was largely removed from the public housing authorities. In 1983, Congress established standard deductions for minors, elderly heads of households, and for other allowable expenses.

Public housing in the United States has never sheltered a significant proportion of Americans, perhaps 3% at most, unlike in many western European countries where 10 to 40% of households, at various income levels, live in state-constructed buildings. But public housing has been a significant part of the debate over American government safety net programs, a significant factor in the history of large American cities over the last 50 years, and cruel disillusionment for social reformers (and many sociologists).

American public housing projects started in the New Deal, accelerated after the war, and then largely stopped in the 1970s, when they were widely described as abject failures. This verdict was hammered home by the well-publicized demolition in 1972 of the Pruitt-Igoe project in St. Louis. Federal support for housing since, skimpy as it is, has largely been in the form of "Section 8" vouchers and dispersed, low-density, mixed housing. The actual number of public housing units has shrunk in recent decades.

In some ways, large-scale public housing was doomed from the start; in other ways, perhaps different critical decisions could have made it work.

26

Building Up, Coming Down

The U.S. began building major projects to house needy families (which should be distinguished from projects to house the elderly) in the 1930s, but the program really took off in the 1950s, creating about one million units by 1973. This was a response to the post-war housing shortage and to many social scientists' view at the time that poor housing itself—crowded, dilapidated quarters—contributed to social dysfunction.

But there were problems right from the start, including the projects' very locations. The authorities put public housing projects, especially those in large cities, disproportionately in poor black neighborhoods. As earlier studies have showed, this was only in part because those neighborhoods had the worst housing and neediest people. In good measure, the politics of class and race decided location; those with the clout to resist low-income neighbors made sure that the construction took place where people who could not resist lived. Another problem at the start was government insistence on holding down construction costs, which would eventually produce problems with upkeep.

Placing large public housing structures in a neighborhood eventually contributed to further decline in the neighborhood. As shown in studies of Chicago and Columbus, Ohio, in the 1960s and '70s, the presence of public housing accentuated local poverty, in part at least because better-off residents moved away.

At the same time, tightening the requirements that housing be provided only to the neediest families meant that stable working-class families, once part of the mix, were gone. The renters became increasingly and exclusively the poorest and most troubled families. Their growing concentration in dense (and tense) settings compounded the problems of order. By 1970, public housing projects had gained their nightmarish image.

One lesson many policy analysts took away from the public housing experiment was that market solutions for housing shortages are better than government ones. Yet, the current Section 8 voucher system has its own problems. Another lesson is that mixed-income housing is preferable. A third is that low-density structures avoid some of the problems. The jury is still out on these ideas.

As many blacks were being packed into the projects like sardines at an alarming rate, they were baited into a trap again by the government. If you were a poor black, in essence you were told *you can rent an apartment not big enough for more than 3–4 people; we will surround you, above you, below you, and on each side of you with another distraught family living under duress, along with about another 100 families in a small area, and put you in the middle of the city. Here is another set up starting you early to get used to living under the same conditions as jail, just without the bars* (some even had bars on the windows). The sad part is that if you were a family and struggled to make a decent living, they would throw you out, stating you make too much to live there even if you paid your rent monthly. In most project housing, it is survival of the fittest; but you become used to it, and you make do with what you have. Some would never know what it's like to live outside of the projects; many blacks were born, raised, and died in these conditions.

27

1994 Crime Bill

―――――――

When Bill Clinton ran for president in 1992, urban black communities across America were suffering from economic collapse. Hundreds of thousands of manufacturing jobs had vanished as factories moved overseas in search of cheaper labor, a new plantation. Globalization and deindustrialization affected workers of all colors but hit African Americans particularly hard.

Unemployment rates among young black men had quadrupled as the rate of industrial employment plummeted. Crime rates spiked in inner-city communities that had been dependent on factory jobs, while hopelessness, despair, and crack addiction swept neighborhoods that had once been solidly working-class. Millions of black folks—many of whom had fled Jim Crow segregation in the South with the hope of obtaining decent work in Northern factories—were suddenly trapped in racially segregated, jobless ghettos.

On the campaign trail, Bill made the economy his top priority and argued persuasively that conservatives were using race to divide the nation and divert attention from the failed economy. In practice, however, he capitulated entirely to the right-wing backlash against the civil rights movement and embraced former President Ronald Reagan's agenda on race, crime, welfare, and taxes—ultimately doing more harm to black communities than Reagan ever did.

We should have seen it coming. Back then, Bill was the standard-bearer for the New Democrats, a group that firmly believed the only way to win back the millions of white voters in the South who had defected to the Republican Party was to adopt the right-wing narrative that black communities ought to be disciplined with harsh punishment rather than coddled with welfare. Reagan had won the presidency by dog-whistling to poor and working-class whites with coded racial appeals: railing against "welfare queens" and criminal "predators" and condemning "big government." Bill aimed to win them back, vowing that he would never permit any Republican to be perceived as tougher on crime than he.

Just weeks before the critical New Hampshire primary, Bill proved his toughness by flying back to Arkansas to oversee the execution of Ricky Ray Rector, a mentally impaired black man who had so little conception of what was about to happen to him that he asked for the dessert from his last meal to be saved for him for later. After the execution, Bill remarked, "I can be nicked a lot, but no one can say I'm soft on crime."

Bill mastered the art of sending mixed cultural messages, appealing to African Americans by belting out "Lift Every Voice and Sing" in black churches while at the same time signaling to poor and working-class whites that he was willing to be tougher on black communities than Republicans had been.

Bill was praised for his no-nonsense, pragmatic approach to racial politics. He won the election and appointed a racially diverse Cabinet that "looked like America." He won re-election four years later, and the American economy rebounded. Democrats cheered. The Democratic Party had been saved. The Clintons won. Guess who lost?

Bill Clinton presided over the largest increase in federal and state prison inmates of any president in American history. He did not declare the war on crime or the war on drugs—those wars were declared before Reagan was elected and long before crack had hit the streets—but he escalated them beyond what many conservatives had imagined possible. He supported the 100-to-1 sentencing disparity for crack vs. powder cocaine, which produced staggering racial injustice in sentencing and boosted funding for drug-law enforcement.

Bill championed the idea of a federal "three strikes" law in his 1994 State of the Union address, months later signed a $30 billion crime bill that created dozens of new federal capital crimes, mandated life sentences for some three-time offenders, and authorized more than $16 billion for state prison grants and the expansion of police forces. The legislation was hailed by mainstream-media outlets as a victory for the Democrats, who "were able to wrest the crime issue from the Republicans and make it their own."

When Bill left office in 2001, the United States had the highest rate of incarceration in the world. Human Rights Watch reported that in seven states, African Americans constituted 80 to 90% of all drug offenders sent to prison, even though they were no more likely than whites to use or sell illegal drugs. Prison admissions for drug offenses reached a level in 2000 for African Americans more than 26 times the level in 1983. All the presidents since 1980 have contributed to mass incarceration, but as Equal Justice Initiative founder Bryan Stevenson recently observed, "President Clinton's tenure was the worst."

Both Clintons now express regret over the crime bill, and Hillary says that she supports criminal-justice reforms to undo some of the damage that was done by her husband's administration. But on the campaign trail, she continues to invoke the economy and the country Bill Clinton left behind as a legacy she would continue.

So what exactly did the Clinton economy look like for black Americans? Taking a hard look at this recent past is about more than just a choice between two candidates. It's about whether or not the Democratic Party can finally reckon with what its policies have done to African American communities and whether it can redeem itself and rightly earn the loyalty of black voters. An oft-repeated myth about the Clinton administration is that although it was overly tough on crime back in the 1990s, at least its policies were good for the economy and for black unemployment rates. The truth is more troubling. As unemployment rates sank to historically low levels for white Americans in the 1990s, the jobless rate among black men in their 20s who didn't have a college degree rose to its highest level ever. This increase in joblessness was propelled by the skyrocketing incarceration rate.

Why is this not common knowledge? Because government statistics like poverty and unemployment rates do not include incarcerated people. As Harvard sociologist Bruce Western explains: "Much of the optimism about declines in racial inequality and the power of the U.S. model of economic growth is misplaced once we account for the invisible poor, behind the walls of America's prisons and jails."

When Bill left office in 2001, the true jobless rate for young, non-college-educated black men (including those behind bars) was 42%. This figure was never reported. Instead, the media claimed that unemployment rates for African Americans had fallen to record lows, neglecting to mention that this miracle was possible only because incarceration rates were now at record highs. Young black men weren't looking for work at high rates during the Clinton era because they were now behind bars—out of sight, out of mind, and no longer counted in poverty and unemployment statistics.

To make matters worse, the federal safety net for poor families was torn to shreds by the Clinton administration in its effort to "end welfare as we know it." In his 1996 State of The Union address, given during his re-election campaign, Bill Clinton declared that "the era of big government is over" and immediately sought to prove it by dismantling the federal welfare system known as Aid to Families With Dependent Children, or AFDC. The welfare-reform legislation that he signed—which Hillary Clinton ardently supported then and characterized as a success as recently as

2008—replaced the federal safety net with a block grant to the states, imposed a five-year lifetime limit on welfare assistance, added work requirements, barred undocumented immigrants from licensed professions, and slashed overall public welfare funding by $54 billion (some was later restored).

Experts and pundits disagree about the true impact of welfare reform, but one thing seems clear: extreme poverty doubled to 1.5 million in the decade and a half after the law was passed. What is extreme poverty? U.S. households are considered to be in extreme poverty if they are surviving on cash incomes of no more than $2 per person per day in any given month. We tend to think of extreme poverty existing in third world countries, but here in the United States, shocking numbers of people are struggling to survive on less money per month than many families spend in one evening dining out. Currently, the United States, the richest nation on the planet, has one of the highest child-poverty rates in the developed world.

Despite claims that radical changes in crime and welfare policy were driven by a desire to end big government and save taxpayer dollars, the reality is that the Clinton administration didn't reduce the amount of money devoted to the management of the urban poor; it changed what the funds would be used for. Billions of dollars were slashed from public housing and child-welfare budgets and transferred to the mass-incarceration machine. By 1996, the penal budget was twice the amount that had been allocated to food stamps. During Bill's tenure, funding for public housing was slashed by $17 billion (a reduction of 61%), while funding for corrections was boosted by $19 billion (an increase of 171%)—"effectively making the construction of prisons the nation's main housing program for the urban poor," according to sociologist Loïc Wacquant.

Bill Clinton championed discriminatory laws against formerly incarcerated people that have kept millions of Americans locked in a cycle of poverty and desperation. The Clinton administration eliminated Pell grants for prisoners seeking higher education to prepare for their release, supported laws denying federal financial aid to students with drug convictions, and signed legislation imposing a lifetime ban on welfare and food stamps for anyone convicted of a felony drug offense—an exceptionally harsh provision given the racially biased drug war that was raging in inner cities.

Perhaps most alarming, Bill also made it easier for public housing agencies to deny shelter to anyone with any sort of criminal history (even an arrest without conviction) and championed the "one strike and you're out" initiative, which meant that families could be evicted from public housing because one member (or a guest) had committed even a minor offense. People released from prison with no money, no job, and nowhere to go could no longer return home to their loved ones living in federally assisted housing without placing the entire family at risk of eviction.

Purging "the criminal element" from public housing played well on the evening news, but no provisions were made for individuals and families as they were forced out on the street. By the end of Bill's presidency, more than half of working-age African American men in many large urban areas were saddled with criminal records and subject to legalized discrimination in employment, housing, access to education, and basic public benefits—relegated to a permanent second-class status eerily reminiscent of Jim Crow.

It is difficult to overstate the damage that's been done. Generations have been lost to the prison system; countless families have been torn apart or rendered homeless; and a school-to-prison pipeline has been born that shuttles young people from their decrepit, underfunded schools to brand-new high-tech prisons.

It didn't have to be like this. As a nation, we had a choice. Rather than spending billions of dollars constructing a vast new penal system, we could have spent those billions putting young people to work in inner-city communities and investing in their schools so that they might have some hope of making the transition from an industrial to a service-based economy. Constructive interventions would have been good not only for African Americans trapped in ghettos but also for blue-collar workers of all colors. At the very least, Democrats could have fought to prevent the further destruction of black communities rather than ratcheting up the wars declared on them.

There are significant racial disparities in sentencing decisions in the United States.

Sentences imposed on Black males in the federal system are nearly 20% longer than those imposed on white males convicted of similar crimes. Black and Latino offenders sentenced in state and federal courts face significantly greater odds of incarceration than similarly situated white offenders and receive longer sentences than their white counterparts in some jurisdictions. Black male federal defendants receive longer sentences than whites arrested for the same offenses and with comparable criminal histories. Research has also shown that race plays a significant role in the determination of which homicide cases result in death sentences.

The racial disparities increase with the severity of the sentence imposed. The level of disproportionate representation of blacks among prisoners who are serving life sentences without the possibility of parole (LWOP) is higher than that among parole-eligible prisoners serving life sentences. The disparity is even higher for juvenile offenders sentenced to LWOP and higher still among prisoners sentenced to LWOP for nonviolent offenses. Although blacks constitute only about 13% of the U.S. population, as of 2009, blacks constitute 28.3% of all lifers, 56.4% of those serving LWOP, and 56.1% of those who received LWOP for offenses committed as a juvenile. As of 2012, the research shows that 65.4% of prisoners serving LWOP for nonviolent offenses are black.

The racial disparities are even worse in some states. In 13 states and the federal system, the percentage of blacks serving life sentences is over 60%. In Georgia and Louisiana, the proportion of blacks serving LWOP sentences is as high as 73.9 and 73.3%, respectively. In the federal system, 71.3% of the 1,230 LWOP prisoners are black.

These racial disparities result from disparate treatment of blacks at every stage of the criminal justice system, including stops and searches, arrests, prosecutions and plea negotiations, trials, and sentencing. Race matters at all phases and aspects of the criminal process, including the quality of representation, the charging phase, and the availability of plea agreements, each of which impact whether juvenile and adult defendants face a potential LWOP sentence. In addition, racial disparities in sentencing can result from theoretically "race neutral" sentencing policies that have significant disparate racial effects, particularly in the cases of habitual offender laws and many drug policies, including mandatory minimums, school zone drug enhancements, and federal policies adopted by Congress in 1986 and 1996 that at the time established a hundred-to-one sentencing disparity between crack and powder cocaine offenses.

Racial disparities in sentencing also result in part from prosecutors' decisions at the initial charging stage, suggesting that racial bias affects the exercise of prosecutorial discretion with respect to certain crimes. One study found that black defendants face significantly more severe charges than whites, even after controlling for characteristics of the offense, criminal history, defense counsel type, age and education of the offender, and the crime rates and economic characteristics of the jurisdiction. Available data also suggest that there are racial disparities in prosecutors' exercise of discretion in seeking sentencing enhancements under three-strikes and other habitual offender laws. For instance, a 1995 legal challenge revealed the racially biased role of prosecutorial discretion in the application of Georgia's two-strikes law. Georgia prosecutors have discretion to decide whether to charge offenders under the state's two-strikes sentencing scheme, which imposes life imprisonment for a second drug offense. They invoked the law against only 1% of white defendants facing a second drug conviction compared to 16% of black defendants. As a result, 98.4% of prisoners serving life sentences under the law were black. In California, studies similarly show that blacks are sentenced under the state's three-strikes law at far higher rates than their white counterparts. Scholars have also noted that federal 851 sentencing enhancements, which at a minimum double a federal drug defendant's mandatory minimum sentence and may raise the maximum sentence from 40 years to life without parole if the defendant has two prior qualifying drug convictions in state or federal courts, are applied by federal prosecutors in an arbitrary and racially discriminatory manner and exacerbate racial disparities in the criminal justice system. While the U.S. Department of Justice and U.S. Sentencing Commission do not develop or publicize data on racial disparities in prosecutors' application of this federal drug sentencing enhancement, the U.S. Sentencing Commission has reported that "black offenders qualified for the 851 enhancement at higher rates than any other racial group."

In general, studies have found that greater racial disparities exist in sentencing for nonviolent crimes, especially property crimes and drug offenses. In particular, there are staggering racial disparities in life-without-parole sentencing for nonviolent offenses. Based on data provided by the U.S. Sentencing Commission and state Departments of Corrections, it is estimated that nationwide, 65.4% of prisoners serving LWOP for nonviolent offenses are black, 17.8% are white, and 15.7% are Latino. According to data collected and analyzed , black prisoners comprise 91.4% of the nonviolent LWOP prison population in Louisiana (the state with the largest number of prisoners serving LWOP for a nonviolent offense), 78.5% in Mississippi, 70% in Illinois, 68.2% in South Carolina, 60.4% in Florida, 57.1% in Oklahoma, and 60% in the federal system.

Blacks constitute a far greater percentage of the nonviolent LWOP population than of the census population as a whole. In the federal system, blacks are 20 times more likely to be sentenced to LWOP for a nonviolent crime than whites. In Louisiana, it was found that blacks were 23 times more likely than whites to be sentenced to LWOP for a nonviolent crime. The racial disparities range from 33 to 1 in Illinois to 18 to 1 in Oklahoma, 8 to 1 in Florida, and 6 to 1 in Mississippi. Blacks are sentenced to life without parole for nonviolent offenses at rates that suggest unequal treatment and that cannot be explained by white and black defendants' differential involvement in crime alone.

There are stark racial disparities in the imposition of life without parole sentences for juvenile offenders in the United States. Nationally, about 77% of juvenile offenders serving LWOP are black and Latino, while black youth are serving these sentences at a rate 10 times higher than white youth. In California—the state with the highest number of prisoners serving LWOP for crimes committed as children—black youth are serving the sentence at a rate that is 18 times higher than the rate for white youth, and Latino youth are sentenced to life without parole five times more than white youth. In Michigan (the state with the second-highest number of such prisoners), while youth of color comprise only 29% of Michigan's children, they are 73% of the state's child offenders serving life without parole. As of 2009, in 14 of the 37 states with people serving LWOP for crimes committed as juveniles, the proportion of African Americans serving that sentence exceeded 65%. Recent research also shows that that the races of victims and offenders may be a factor in determining which juvenile offenders are sentenced to life without parole, as black youth with a white victim are far more likely to be sentenced to life without parole than white youth with a black victim. The percentage of black juvenile offenders serving LWOP for the homicide of a white victim (43.4%) is nearly twice the rate at which black juveniles are arrested for suspected homicide of a white person (23.2%). In contrast, white juvenile offenders with black victims are only about half as likely (3.6%) to be sentenced to LWOP for the homicide crime as their proportion of arrests for suspected homicide of a black victim (6.4%). These outcomes are the result of racial biases that affect who is arrested, who is detained, and who receives the harshest punishments. For example, a 1990 statistical evaluation of police intake decisions in five Michigan counties revealed that, even when controlling for other statistically significant factors such as drug charges, weapons possession, or prior convictions, "race continued to exert an independent and significant influence on detention...[while] youth of color were more likely to be charged with more serious offenses, they were also more likely to be detained independent of offense seriousness."

Since 1970, the prison population in America has gone from around 259,000 inmates to more than 3,000,000 today. The destruction of this many black families will cause havoc among the black communities for generations to come. As black men face 5 to 50 year sentences for a first-time offense, their families at home struggle to survive and stay afloat.

28

Mental Slavery

Mental Slavery is far more sinister than physical slavery, because the chains are invisible and are transmitted across generations.

If African slavery was only physical, African people would have within one generation been able to skip the plethora of social-economic issues which plague African people globally the second the chains came off. Slavery and other institutionalized forms of targeted race-based oppression have caused certain symptoms of dysfunction in the African community, which has been reinforced in each generation. The legacy of slavery has promoted and nursed the direct association between being African and being inferior—between being African and being unequal, incapable, and less worthy. It also promotes ways of thinking that continue to impede growth and development, such as cultivating dependence and reactive behaviors, being more content to be at best an observer complaining about the world as opposed to being a change agent in the world, and being content to be history's permanent victim. Every possible solution is dismissed with yet another trite excuse. Mental slavery affects how people see their own reality. This manipulation has always been through mainstream media, religion, and education. So the opinions about reality are sourced—without any suspicion—from the very same people that said Africa was bursting with primitive cannibal savages, a place of no history, a place of no humanity—the dark and savage continent. And via these mass indoctrination devices the very same imperialistic colonial powers are still (without change in strategy) stating that *without Western "help" you have no hope; our ways are the best ways, our goods are the best goods, and our "human rights" (aka quest for more oil) are good for you; you are better off with us than with your own people.* People remain gullible to the "gospel" of their former enslavers—despite all the sordid history in evidence. So the root of mental slavery is ignorance, resulting in a poor grasp of information about self and the world, preventing functioning to one's full human potential. When someone is mentally enslaved, he does not understand that the guys dressed in fire protection gear, with fire hoses, breaking down their door to rescue them from the fire are saving them. That is why mental slavery is worse than physical slavery. Because at least during physical slavery, if you were to get on board the slave ship and break the chains and take the people back to Africa, they would all thank you and call you a liberator. Today, trying to free people who are mentally enslaved, you get called names while they run away from you, and deeper into oppression. It is critical that we understand the slave mind, not the slave mouth. You can train someone to say anything; they can say "I am 100% for transforming African people," but deep inside the mind is that little slave who only wants "a more comfortable cage." So when African agency and African economics hit reality, they freeze up and go into slave attack mode to preserve the cage environment.

During slavery, the scraps and leftovers of food and apparel went to the enslaved Africans. Today, the crumbs and the fat from the used bones of Western propaganda are still staples of the diet of the subaltern; blind allegiance to a system that has no recourse to any sort of higher human values; copied, aped, celebrated, and applied by free men and women under "independent" flags and anthems all over the world; almost oblivious to their re-applying the machinery of oppression.

What being oppressed means in the broadest and most salient terms is the occupation of ethics, logic, culture, thought process, long term thinking, critical thinking, and paradigms by those of the oppressor's. So the beauty standard which is applicable to the European aesthetic is transferred, without modification, regardless of the incongruous state of beauty that is, to the oppressed. These models of beauty are desperately adopted—at all cost. Mental slavery created an inability to make reference to self, so that in both the contemporary and historical context identities, even those under the banner of "liberation," are corrupted and sit upon the very platform of their oppressors paradigms, for the benefit of that oppression. Liberation within the structures that created the African 'Other" is therefore relative—not absolute.

The discourse on post-traumatic slavery syndrome is part of the study of mental slavery. While that study looks for biological connectivity to the genetic ancestors of African people, this study reports on patterns in human behavior, including economics, socialization, formal and informal relationships, ideology, work ethos, and all other related areas of people's activity, more than the film Roots, of lives on a plantation exposed to inhumanities. The most violent product of chattel slavery is mental slavery. It expresses itself by creating, among other things, dependency and an inferiority complex. It infects every concept from notions of beauty, values, and even the preference of "renting" over the prospect of "buying." Many Africans globally, especially in areas heavily influenced by European domination, continue to wear their wealth on the outside (shoes, clothing, cars), while other groups wear their money on the inside (educational development) first. Mental slavery also impacts African discernment. Because failure to know oneself also means failure to identify self-interest, it is often in this confused state the offense of oppression cannot be located in the minds of the mental slaves. It is no wonder they are given to attack the seat of their own liberation for minutial issues. In chattel slavery, Africans could not own anything; you could not have long-term investment plans in your family (they could be sold away at any moment). Myopic thinking is a ves-tige of slavery, as no enslaved African had the luxury for over 300 years of thinking beyond the moment. So today a flashy car (instant gratification) takes the place of any long-term wealth (like owning a house). The need to sate the superficial is not exclusively created by mental enslavement but is heavily augmented by it.

Investment in education was futile in slavery and still this legacy continues. Mental slavery also impacts most of all value of self, value in seeing African stories. How else can we explains why the Jewish story in film and print is everywhere in the world despite Jews only being a world population less than the city of Lagos.

And why is it that the story of Africa (more than one billion peo-ple) is rarely told, and when it is told it is at the hands of Euro-pean agents. Some Africans are so mentally confused that they are active agents of whitewashing and escaping from slavery, and they will state "I am sick of hearing about slavery; the past is the past." The African voice, the African woman and man, the African rela-tionships and African films and media have no value in the minds of those who have no value of self. And this pervasive legacy washes over not only this contemporary African generation but future generations yet to be born.

29

The Current Climate

We know by now that America is run as a corporation; we know it claims a democracy, but stands as a republic (to the Republic for which it stands). We have all said this before, pledging allegiance to a country set up to oppress us forever. As little white boys and girls run around dancing, singing, dressing, and imitating blacks, America is confused. How could we spend all these years degrading these people, only for our children to want to be like them? The light will always shine through in God's people; there is nothing that can stop our progress.

Being black in America is like running a race with hurdles, except instead of 3.5 feet like everyone else's, our hurdles are 6 feet. Yes, the race is fixed so that we lose.

Although we have had all these obstacles, we have still made progress in America. Since the early years, blacks have been

---

instrumental in inventions such as the brush and comb, the foun-
tain pen, the clothes dryer, the traffic light, and many more. Music
is dominated by Hip Hop, which was created by blacks; it is extra-
ordinary to take words from a foreign language to create your
own language within a language. Hip Hop is a multi-billion dollar
industry that spans the whole globe, and it is sad that the majority
of the money that is made goes into white pockets.

African Americans dominate sports, we are genetically superior
athletes, and it shows, even in the Olympics. Yes, we are sent to
represent for America, and upon winning an event you have to
stand and pledge allegiance to the same flag that represents the
murdering and enslaving of our ancestors.

There are huge entrepreneurs who have dominated the hair care,
magazine, trade, retail and grocery, and book industries and
almost every other industry you can imagine. We also have prominent actors, directors and producers, and business men and
women as well as dominant roles in the military, school systems,
and police and fire departments, not to mention lawyers, judges,
doctors, journalists, and many in the financial community.

We have achieved all of these milestones even with poor schools
systems in our community, an unjust criminal system targeted to
jail us long-term for profits, degraded housing systems, limited
job opportunities, and no resources for aiding with education for
blacks to take advantage of.

Police are killing young blacks at an alarming rate. It is shown
over and over again on T.V. for everyone to see, and nearly none
are convicted of criminal charges. Moreover, we are targeted by

the media and press for marching for justice. Crime sentences for blacks are still much higher than for whites, and even if the punishment for convictions were to become equal, it will always be unequal if you have a high-priced lawyer who can pay his golf buddy judge for a lenient verdict.

We have achieved a black president. Sounds great, but only to have congress shoot down 90% of his changes, and have his family the target of racial jokes and made a mockery of. White Americans even feel like they are entitled to whomever they feel should be in the white house just because one African American became POTUS. This is no more relevant than the current elections—either way blacks will be at a disadvantage with the next one who gains office.

30

What Should Be Done?

A psychiatrist once said for every negative thought it takes 17 positives thoughts to even your mental state. With this being said, after 400 years of oppression, there is no way that with 150 years of not being in bondage we are not affected mentally in a negative way today.

Black people in America must first make a conscious effort to want more for themselves, their communities, and their families. It will start at home, teaching children to grow and own their own business, create and invent things to help current issues in their neighborhoods, and educate themselves on black history and not just what is strategically taught in schools. We must remain with a chip on our shoulder. We were never taught to band together, because since they brought us over here they intentionally divided us, and it still remains in our psychological DNA. Killing each other and publically shaming your fellow dark- or light-skinned people have to cease. We must band together; all the hate against your fellow brother or sister out of jealousy and/or envy must stop. Each one teach one; we must begin to organize locally to make huge strides nationally. Talk to your neighbors; create community organizations that will plan to induct change.

In America, black families do not commit to anything on a daily or weekly basis with the exception of work or church in most cases, which is not a bad thing, but there must be a daily commitment to inspire change. The government is like a big pyramid, with the POTUS being the one center block on top and funneling down from there. To really make a change, we must challenge the pyramid from the bottom, voting locally for politicians who will dedicate their time to promoting change for our inner city schools, housing, hospitals, and small business opportunities. As we begin to vote who want in at the bottom, slowly it will affect the next level and the next level and so on until we are high enough to take action permanently. Think of it like a large corporation, the CEO is so far removed from the everyday worker at the bottom that most of the problems the lower worker complains about will never really get addressed, because you have supervisors, managers, secretaries, vice presidents, and a bunch of others in the chain that handle most issues. It is the same with the government: the people at the top can never really address our issues if they have never been through our issues and are unfamiliar with them; anyone close to the top is only thinking of making more money at the expense of the frontline workers or the slaves. If you have ever worked at a job for more than 10 years, you will know that change is always happening, but it always leads to more work for you without extra pay, or with pay cuts or downgrades, while for most people in higher positions, their conditions and pay will usually increase.

Amongst all the public killings by police officers within our nation, it has to be determined that we must decide who can police our neighborhoods. The officers in most inner cities are scared, and when you are scared you tend to pull the trigger a lot faster. Police in our communities should be from our communities, raised in our communities; they must know and be able to relate to the people and have the ability to defuse tensions before they arise. There was a time when police knew the local deli owner, their kids went to the same schools, and they walked the beat with pride and without fear because he or she took pride in maintaining a level of safety where they grew up. When you take a white officer who only knows about black communities from the T.V. and newspapers and throw him in to police an inner city housing project, the very site of 10 young black boys with hoodies walking toward him will send fear through his body. It is a natural reaction; he will tend to react more aggressively than someone who may know them all by names and as a basketball team, not a gang. This is not the officers fault; it is the system. They purposely place young renegades wanting to make a name for themselves in select places, hoping to break up any bond or relationships that may have been developed by black officers.

We must fight to determine the curriculum that is being taught in our schools. Our children are taught to work hard in school, grow up, and get a job, while white children are taught to do well in school, go to college, open a business, and hire blacks to work for you at minimum wage. The world has changed since the current curriculum that is taught in inner cities was developed in the early '60s. The education system teaches our kids basic math, reading and English, some science and world history, Washington, Lincoln, etc. In most cases, the things discussed within those walls will not help you to progress in the real world. Young black children at an early age need to be taught about business, entrepreneurship, finance, real estate, politics, law, and African American history. There are more things to spark the young bring besides the great efforts of Martin Luther King, Jr., and Marcus Garvey, and Malcom X. A young mind is too vital in this day and age to waste; schools should teach practices such as religion, discipline, goals, and how to build and run a business online and offline. Kids need to know the direct coalition of our history, how it effects them and their families today, and how to change things for their kids and families in the future.

The revolution must continue. Blacks control and dominate a large part of the U.S. economy; statistically we spend the most (we being middle class and down), which is strange. There comes a time when you have to give up the plague of labels and branding and decide that your hard-earned dollars are worth more than a logo on your shirt or high-priced sneakers. If there is anything to really learn from white Americans it is that clothes are the last thing you should spend the majority of your money on. Fancy cars, jewelry and clothes are just masks to hide low self-esteem. Invest in appreciating assets, and don't spend on things that depreciate. Your dollars and self-worth should be at the forefront of your priorities and for generations after you. Take some of your dollars and save them, invest in a business for yourself and your family, and be smart about your tactics and don't let the world know your every action on social media. Look for black-owned banks and businesses to spend your dollars; and donate to black colleges, black charities, and black functions. And if you don't feel comfortable donating to strangers, get together with some people and help organize a charity to help in your community. It is never too late to educate yourself on business; most do not know that it takes less than $400 to start your own online business, and that includes a trademark, tax i.d. number, website, and small marketing. Support one another and align yourself with like-minded people who want more out of life and want to be able to pass down finance and knowledge for generations.

Did You Know?

- Immigrants have more freedom and access to loans for businesses than black Americans. Immigrants are found to have higher business ownership and formation rates than non-immigrants. Roughly one 1 of 10 immigrant workers owns a business and 620 of 100,000 immigrants (0.62%) start a business each month.

- Immigrant-owned businesses start with higher levels of startup capital than non-immigrant-owned businesses.

- Nearly 20% of immigrant-owned businesses started with $50,000 or more in startup capital, compared with 15.9% of non-immigrant-owned businesses.

- Roughly two-thirds of immigrant-owned businesses report that the most common source of startup capital is personal or family savings. Other commonly reported sources of startup capital by immigrant businesses are credit cards, bank loans, personal or family assets, and home equity loans. Overall, the sources of startup capital used by immigrant businesses do not differ substantially from those used by non-immigrant firms.

- Businesses owned by immigrants have an average sales level of $435,000, roughly 70% of the average sales level of non-immigrant firms.

- Immigrant-owned businesses are slightly more likely to hire employees than are non-immigrant-owned firms; however, they tend to hire fewer employees on average.

- Immigrant-owned businesses are more likely to export their goods and services. Among immigrant businesses, 7.1% export compared with only 4.4% for non-immigrant businesses.

- Entrepreneurship increases with maturity, and married people are more likely to start a business.

- More generally, there is a U-shaped relationship between entrepreneurship and education. Entrepreneurship rates are lower for high school graduates than for high school dropouts, but entrepreneurship rates are similar between those with some college and high school graduates. College graduates have higher rates of entrepreneurship, and those with graduate degrees have the highest rates of entrepreneurship.

- Among immigrants, 52.1% own a home compared with 70.8% of non-immigrants.

- The proof is there that they are more easily funded, because they are more willing to contribute to export and import trades, whereas black Americans have no country to import and/or export to. Yet, this does not mean that we cannot own, operate, and run a fully functional and profitable business. They do not want us to keep our money in our communities when it is better spent in their pockets. Keep your eyes open.

Last but not least, African Americans must combine to determine how to become non-citizens of the United States. If citizens of the United States cannot sue their country and demand equal rights and reparations for our ancestors, then we may be better off as U.S. nationals, or diplomats, or legal non-citizens, because we did not voluntarily come to this country. We can bring America up on war crimes charges and eventually get, if not for us, then for future generations, the promise of a free country with a justice system for all, equal jobs, education, and housing. Most blacks love America as a country (the land is great), but the people who write and make unjust laws and enforce bureaucratic policies to maintain a lower level for a population of people has to change to prevent another Civil War. Some may argue that America wants these things to happen to push forward a New World Order, which would make things even harder for non-whites in this country. The government can no longer move forward with a deaf ear to people who are crying out for change and who are not asking for handouts but rather just asking for what is owed to them from our ancestors work in an imbalanced and biased racial slave force.

Band together people, do your part in making America a place where we have a voice, and demand a change in our conditions—legally, institutionally, in labor, housing, and education. As much as they would never say it, they will thank us for it eventually.